AF477611

ABNOE

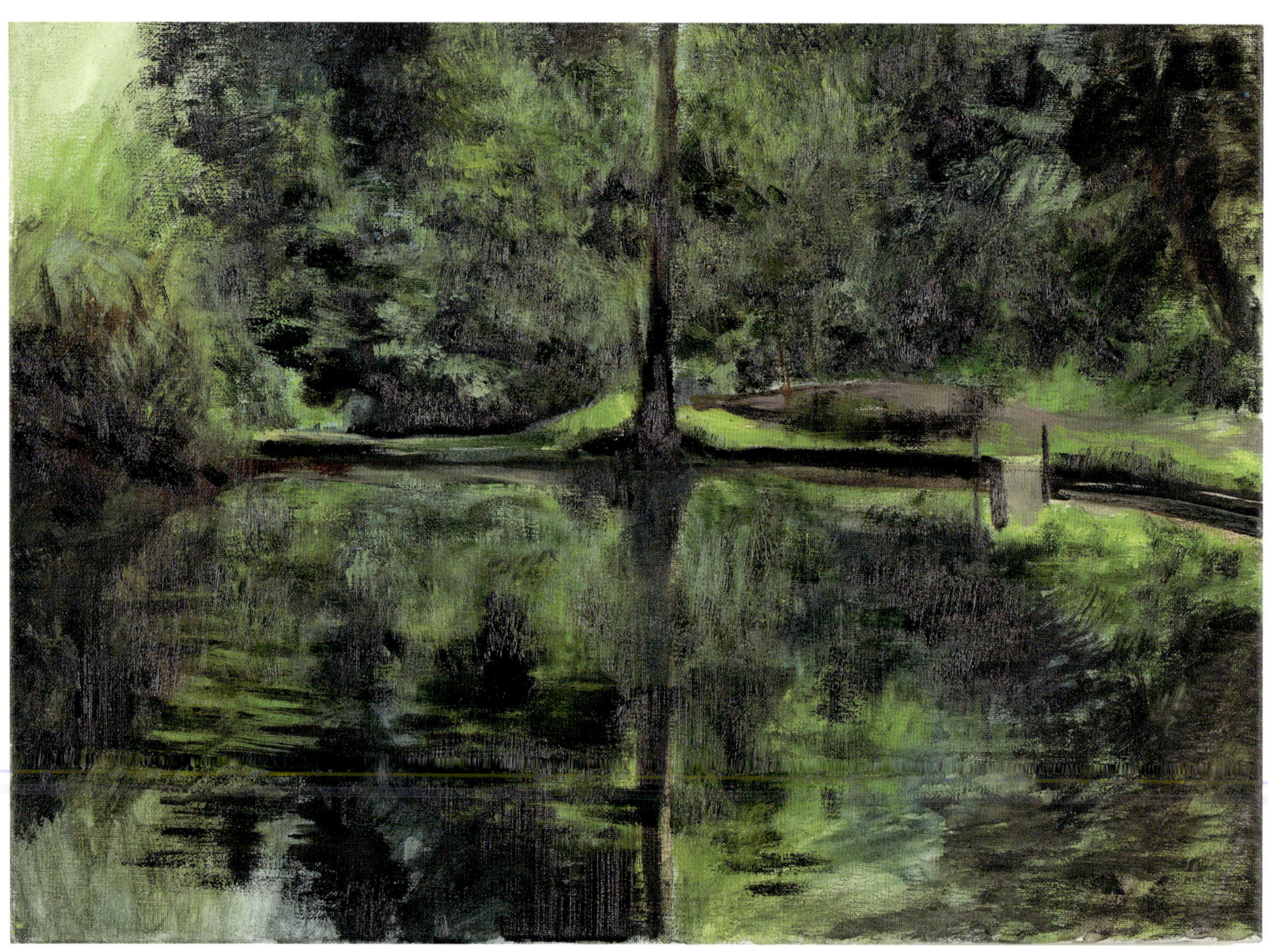

Stift
2008
30 x 40 cm

Alexander Raymond

ABNOE

KERBER EDITION YOUNG ART

Dank an:

die Kulturbehörde Hamburg, Ingrid Baireuther
die HHLA, LEVY Galerie, Alexander Sairally,
Prof. Werner Hunstein, Andreas Breitbart
SKAM e. V.

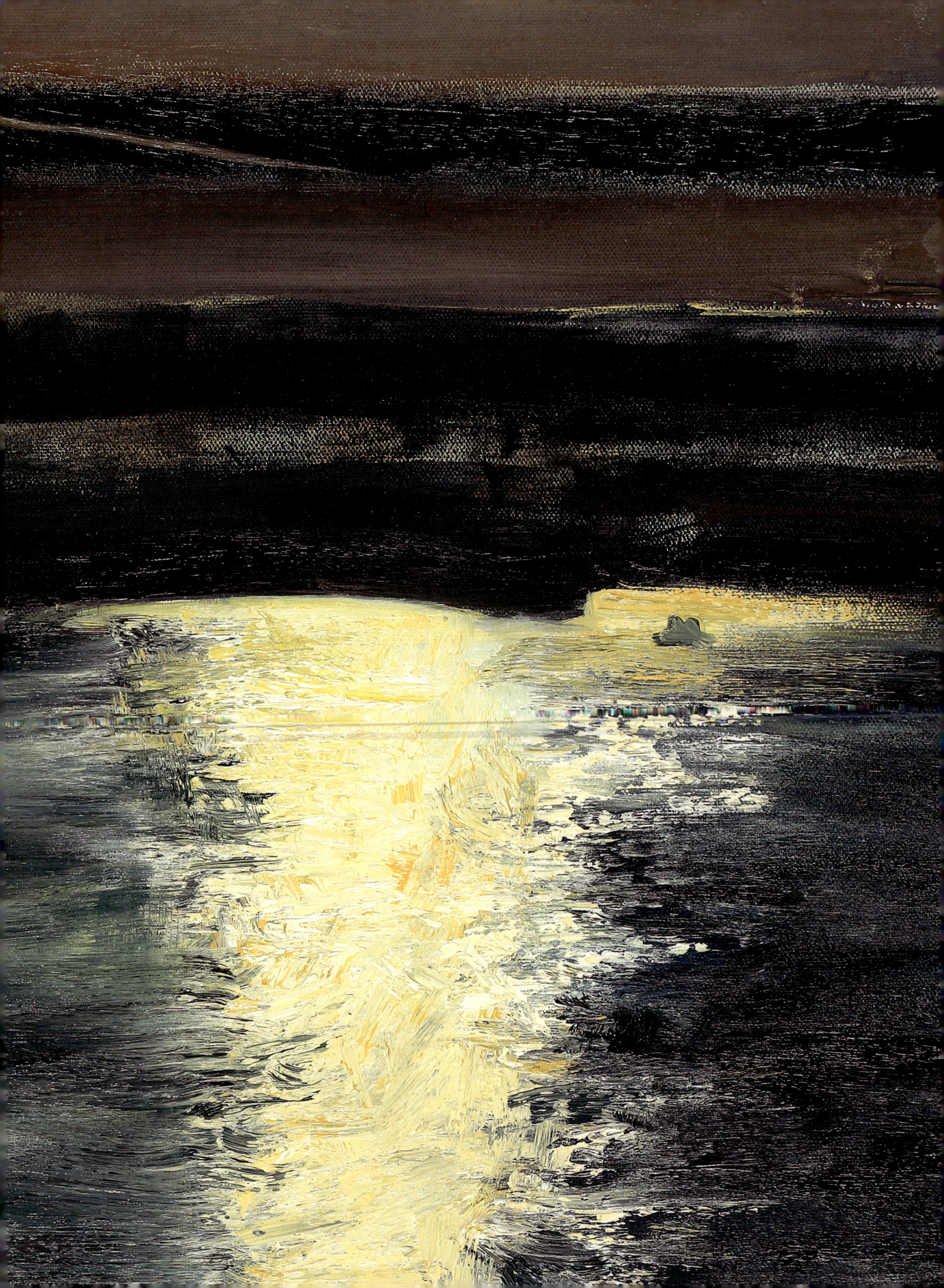

Alexander Raymond
Magie-Logik

Die Vorliebe von Menschen für Behausungen am Hang mit Seeblick – idealtypisch ist es der Blick über die Savanne – luxuriös einleuchtend der Blick aus dem Wintergarten einer Villa über eine mit lockeren Baumgruppen bestandene Rasenfläche hinab zum See oder Fluss, so wie etwa in den Elbvororten, diese Vorliebe ist von dem Anthropologen Fritz Kramer in einem Aufsatz als Habitatvorliebe beschrieben worden, einer Vorliebe aller Menschen, deren ursprünglichen Lebensraum man sich in einer solchen Savannenlandschaft vorstellen muss. Sodass allerlei ideale Wohnanlagen also immer die sehr lange zurückreichenden Erinnerungen an eben diese Ideallandschaft in sich bergen. Ein pazifizierendes Moment, das neben allen auffälligen Unterschieden der Kulturen doch immerhin eine Gemeinsamkeit in der Art und Weise der gemeinsamen Behausung der Welt ausweist: Hanglage mit Seeblick.

Das kontemplative Starren auf Wasserflächen, was einst dem geschützten Warten auf das Auftauchen des zu jagenden Wilds gegolten haben mag, ist für Nicht-Villenbesitzer im Englischen Landschaftspark, beim Spazieren entlang der Elbe, außerdem in jeder Bierwerbung und nicht zu vergessen allen Schmonzetten in Bild und Text zu erfahren, Fritz Kramer geht so weit zu sagen, dass sich auch der Mietskasernenbewohner mit einem Aquarium in eine solche Situation versetzt. Sei's drum. Es ist immer das gleiche Phänomen zu beobachten, Menschen aller Länder schauen beharrlich ins Weite.

Die Spiegelung einer solchen Fläche, sei es zur Selbstbeschau, Meditation oder was auch immer die aktuelle ideologische Befrachtung sein mag, die Weite ist das, was man von so einer Hanglage mit Seeblick aus sieht. Dieses Motiv taucht in den Malereien von Alexander Raymond als spiegelnde Fensterfront auf. Gleich einer Wasserfläche, auf die man am Wochenende zu seiner Erholung schaut, die Augen auf unendlich gedreht. Diese Fensterspiegelflächen in den Bildern Alexander Raymonds sind kein konstruiertes Arrangement, sondern formieren den speziellen Grad zwischen Magie und Logik, dem seine Bilder gewidmet sind. Die logische Weise lautet: Diese Fenster

Alexander Raymond
Magic logic

People's predilection for dwelling on hillsides overlooking the water – in ideal terms a view across the savannah – the luxuriously radiant view from a villa's conservatory across a grassy plain dotted with scattered clumps of trees towards a lake or river, as in Hamburg's suburbs along the Elbe River. In an essay, Anthropologist Fritz Kramer described this preference as a preferred habitat, a preference of all people, whose original living areas one must imagine as being this type of savannah landscape. Thus all ideal residential locations harbour ancient memories of precisely these ideal landscapes. A pacifying aspect, which besides all obvious differences between cultures still exhibits a similarity in the world's most universal style of accommodation: a hillside location overlooking the water.

Staring contemplatively across expanses of water, which may once have been related to lying in concealment while waiting for the appearance of game to be hunted, can be experienced – even by people who don't own villas in English landscape gardens – in every beer advertisement, not to mention all kitschy works of image and text. Fritz Kramer goes so far as to say that even tenement inhabitants use aquariums to set themselves into this type of situation. Be that as it may. The same phenomenon can be observed everywhere, as people from every land gaze insistently into the distance.

The reflection from such a surface, be it for introspection, meditation or whatever else the current ideological climate may dictate; the distance is that which one can see from just this type of hillside location with a view of the water. This motif appears in the paintings of Alexander Raymond as a reflective window surface. It is like an expanse of water onto which one gazes on weekends for relaxation, eyes turned towards infinity. These reflective window surfaces in Alexander Raymond's paintings are no construed arrangement, but instead form the particular intersection between magic and logic to which his pictures are dedicated. The logical side is this: These windows can in fact be found on Raymond's habitat, his studio at the end of a busy and lively street in Hamburg, yet with the best view, which is the magical component: pro-

befinden sich tatsächlich an Raymonds Habitat, seinem Atelier am Ende einer stark befahrenen und belebten Straße in Hamburg, mit bestem Ausblick aber, und das ist die magische Komponente: geschützt vor dem allabendlichen Amüsierbetrieb, nämlich darüber hinaus gehoben, sodass man von dort oben wie aus einer tiefen Höhle in einer Steinwand blickt, die dem Passanten verborgen bleibt, weil die Scheiben von außen nahezu blind vor Dreck sind, von innen aber als Zauberspiegel funktionieren, auf dem sich Szenen zeigen, die nicht aus dem Raum stammen, aus dem hinaus man in den Spiegel schaut. Dieses ganze Gequatsche über Spiegelungen erklärt pragmatisch, warum Raymonds Motive zu allermeist Nachtszenen darstellen, da sich nur bei Dunkelheit der beleuchtete Arbeitsraum in die nächtliche Szenerie der Feuerwerke und Leuchtreklamen vor dem Fenster hineinspiegelt.

Diese Schemen, sind für Raymond, der auch einmal Vor- und Frühgeschichte studierte, denn auch Spiegelungen durch Epochen, malerische wie Erdzeitalter. Was macht der Mandrill neben dem schweren Brokatvorhang? Ein malerisches Zitat, das an holländische Genremalerei, an die Faszination der täuschenden Wiedergabe des Stofflichen erinnert, und ein entwicklungsgeschichtliches Zitat. Und wo ist eigentlich die Frau mit der Fellmütze, die man im Fenster sieht – denn der Platz auf dem Sofa im Raum ist leer. Die Zeiten in Raymonds Bildern sind mühelos zu überbrücken beim Blick in die spiegelnden Fensterflächen. Seine Motive, auch ohne die Spiegelebene bereits lange eingeführt als magisches Bildrepertoire: Fell, schlafende Frauen, ein Fuchs, Irrlichter, sind immer Teil einer Formation, die wie zu einer schamanistischen Orakelveranstaltung angeordnet sind, ein bisschen unordentlich auf den ersten Blick, aber absolut notwendig für den Zaubereffekt.

Nora Sdun

tected from the nightly crowds of amusement seekers, namely raised up out of them, so that one looks out from up there as from a deep cave in a wall of stone remaining hidden to passersby, because from the outside the panes of glass are almost completely coated with grime, but from the inside they work like a magic mirror displaying scenes not originating in the room from which one gazes into the mirror. All this talk about reflections explains pragmatically why Raymond's motifs generally depict night scenes, because only in darkness is the lighted workroom reflected in the nightly scenery of fireworks and neon signs outside the window.

For Raymond, who once also studied pre- and early history, these spectres are then also reflections through the ages, as picturesque as geological eras. What is the mandrill doing next to the heavy brocade curtain? It is a painterly citation, reminiscent of Dutch genre painting and the fascination of illusionistically rendered fabrics, and an evolutionary quotation. And where indeed is the woman with the fur cap, who one sees in the window – for the space on the sofa in the room is empty. The times in Raymond's pictures can be easily traversed by a glance in the reflecting window's surface. His motifs, even without the reflective level, have already long since been introduced as a magical pictorial repertory. Fur, sleeping women, a fox, will-o-the-wisps: these are always part of a formation that seem to have been allocated to a shamanistic oracular event: a little disordered at first glance, but absolutely necessary for the magical effect.

Nora Sdun
(Translation: Sean Gallagher)

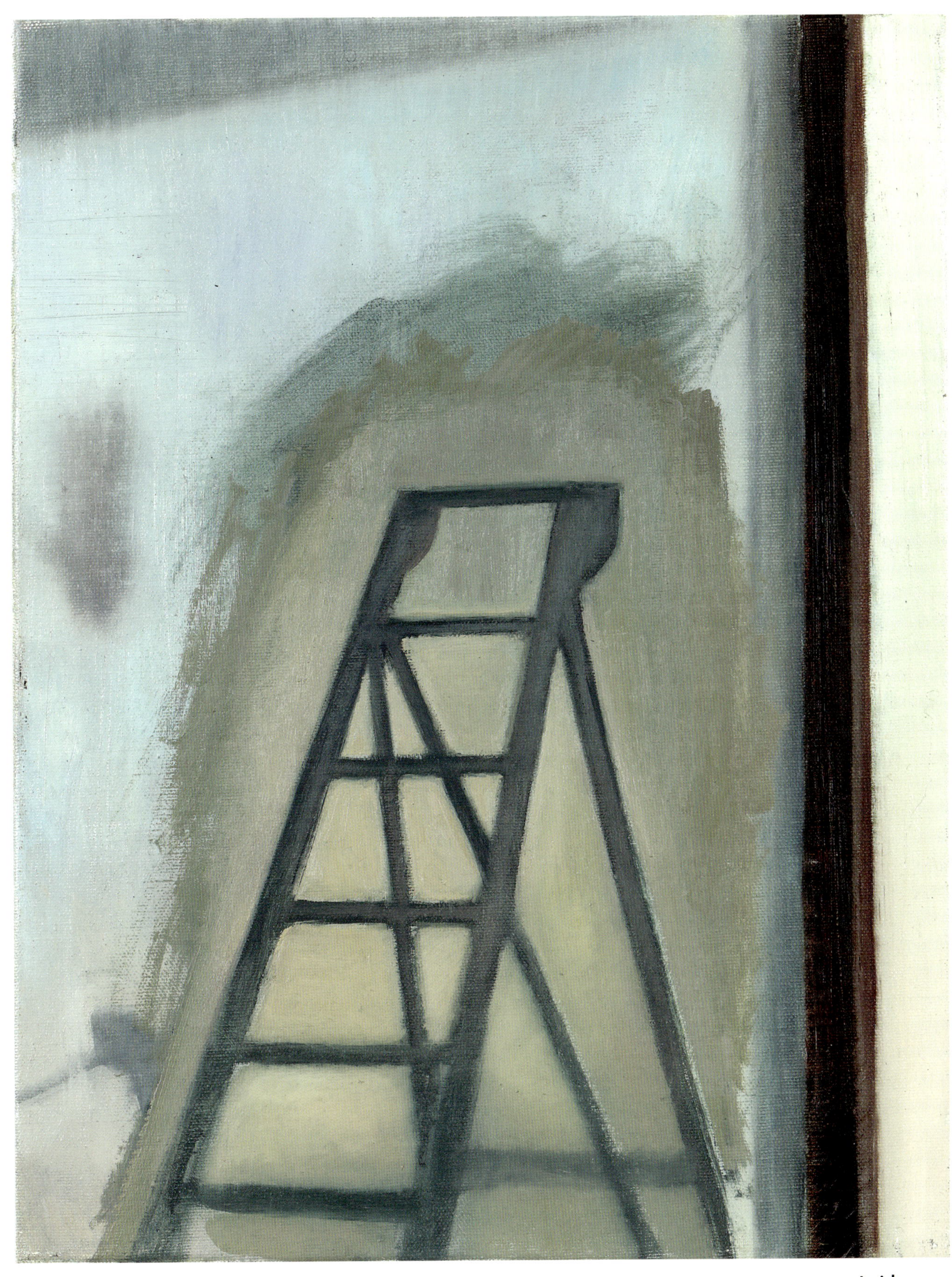

Leider
2007
40 x 30 cm

„...das Naheliegende ist auch das Unwahrscheinliche."
Malerei von Alexander Raymond

Das grüne, in eine Raumecke gerückte Sofa wirkt ziemlich durchgesessen. Unter einem der Kissen ragt ein heller Stofffetzen hervor. An der blassen Wand dahinter hängt ein kleiner, weiß gefranster Bildteppich mit Bergmotiv und Steinbockherde sowie ein amorphes Etwas in leuchtendem Orange, womöglich ringartig gerollter Kupferdraht. Im Vordergrund fällt der abgenutzte Teppichboden ins Auge, ebenfalls orange und kleinteilig gemustert. Darauf ein Fuchs, der gerade aus dem Blickfeld zu schleichen scheint und dessen vordere Hälfte vom Bildrand abgeschnitten ist. Vermutlich ausgestopft. Links nimmt eine matt reflektierende, raumhohe Fensterscheibe knapp zwei Drittel des Bildes ein und ist nach Wand und Boden hin durch braune Balken eingefasst, so dass sie wie ein gerahmtes Gemälde wirkt. Im Glas spiegelt sich das Szenario, ein Bild im Bild, das die Verdopplung der Raumansicht aus leicht verschobener Perspektive wiedergibt. Von links ragt schräg ein Stückchen schwarzes Tuch ins Blickfeld, das einem hier wie ein fallender Vorhang erscheinen könnte. Eine Anspielung, vielleicht – im Zweifel aber nicht mehr und nicht weniger als ein Element, das sich in den abstrakten Rhythmus der Bildformen einfügt, ihn kontort und weiter forciert. Das großformatige Electrick (2008) [Abb. S. 49] wirkt auf den ersten Blick recht karg, ist aber kompositionell stark durchgearbeitet. Das Interieur verblüfft durch eine ganz eigene Art monumentaler Beiläufigkeit, atmosphärisch schwebt die Darstellung zwischen Stilisierung und Momentaufnahme, alles wirkt daran sehr eingelebt und dennoch merkwürdig künstlich, wie eingefroren oder stillgestellt.

Die semantische Grundierung durch lapidar Alltägliches ist typisch für die Arbeit Alexander Raymonds, und auch, wie er dies dann im malerischen Prozess auf subtile Stilisierung hin zuspitzt. „Es ist das Merkmal aller meiner Bilder", sagt er, „dass sie auf einer Idee von Inszenierung basieren, sich dann aber doch zufällig entwickeln."(1) Das Verhältnis von konzeptueller Bildidee und prozessualer Offenheit der Umsetzung gibt seiner Arbeit ihre besondere Prägung. Auch wenn Bildaufbau und Arrangement in Grundzügen meist von Beginn an feststehen, vieles und

"...the obvious is also the improbable."
Paintings by Alexander Raymond

The green sofa that has been pushed into the corner of the room looks rather worn. A light-coloured scrap of cloth juts out from beneath one of the cushions. A small, white, fringed tapestry with mountain scenery and a herd of ibex is hanging on the pale wall behind, along with something amorphous in bright orange, possibly a roll of copper wire. In the foreground, the threadbare wall-to-wall carpeting stands out. It is also orange and has a detailed pattern. There is a fox on the carpet that seems to skulk out of the scene, its front half is cut off by the edge of the picture. Probably stuffed. To the left, a frosted floor-to-ceiling window takes up almost two thirds of the scenario and is enclosed by brown beams along the floor and walls, giving it the appearance of a framed image. The scene is mirrored in the glass, a picture within a picture that reflects the doubling of the view of the room from a slight shift in perspective. From the left, a slanted piece of black cloth pushes into the line of vision like a falling curtain. An allusion perhaps – however in case of doubt it is no more and no less than an element which blends into the abstract rhythm of the picture shape, countering and emphasising it. The large format painting Electrick (2008) [fig. p. 49] creates a rather sparse impression at first glance, however compositionally it is very sophisticated. The interior perplexes the viewer with its own unique, monumental incidentality while atmospherically the depiction hovers between a stylised image and a snapshot. Everything about it appears established and yet strangely artificial, as if frozen or immobilized.

The semantic background created by succinct everyday scenes and objects is typical of Alexander Raymond's work and also of the way in which he causes it to culminate in subtle stylisation during the process of painting. "It is characteristic of all my paintings," he says "that they are based on the concept of orchestration yet still develop randomly." (1) The relationship between the conceptual idea behind the picture and the process-related openness of the implementation gives his work its special character. Even if the basic composition of the picture and arrangement are usually determined from the start, many ele-

letztlich das Entscheidende fließt während des Malens ins Bild ein. Seine motivischen Ausgangspunkte findet Raymond im „Naheliegenden", wie er es nennt. Das heißt, er greift auf Settings aus seinem unmittelbaren Umfeld zu. Das können Ateliersituationen oder ein Blick aus dem Fenster ebenso sein wie stillebenhafte Arrangements im Studio. Auch für Electrick hat Raymond eine solche „Versuchsanordnung" vorgenommen. Er betont allerdings, es gehe ihm da nicht so sehr um die Orte oder Gegenstände selbst – insoweit jedenfalls, als es genauso gut auch andere Orte und Objekte sein könnten. Er nimmt, was da ist und ihm für Bildideen passend scheint, und das ist praktisch all das, was er dort vorfindet, wo er sich aufhält. Meist eben im Atelier: „Ich lasse mich schon inspirieren vom Alltäglichem", sagt er, „das ist mal das Sofa, Wandbilder, Kissen und so weiter. Dinge, die einfach da sind. Inzwischen ist schon ein gewisser Fundus entstanden. Es ist ja so: Ich komme hier rein, es ist eigentlich ein beliebiger Raum. Ich gehe davon aus, da vier oder sechs Stunden zu verbringen. In diesem Zeitraum wird irgendetwas passieren. Davon kann man ausgehen. Wie wenn man die ganze Zeit aus dem Fenster schaut, man wird Dinge sehen, die vollkommen abwegig sind."

Oft stellen sich die Arrangements bei Raymond also ganz von selber ein. Ein Beispiel dafür ist das Foto, das als Vorlage für Orakel (2008) [Abb. S. 29] diente und das sich einer besonderen Situation verdankt. Darauf ist die räumliche Situation von Überlagerungen geprägt: In der Spiegelung des Fensters vermischen sich Feuerwerk, Nachthimmel, Fotoblitz und Atelierwand, verschmelzen zu einem dunkel lichtdurchtränkten Innen-Außen, das nicht mehr klar zu unterscheiden ist. „Ursprünglich wollte ich etwas ganz anderes malen", so Raymond. „Es gab nur eine vage Idee vom Ineinandergreifen des Gegenüberliegenden. Dann ging plötzlich das Feuerwerk los, und das wurde für mich sofort zum Thema. Ich habe das Licht ausgeschaltet und war fasziniert davon, wie sich im Atelierraum alles spiegelte. Das hatte ich so noch nie zuvor gesehen. Meine Bildideen entstehen oft auf diese Weise." Was sich in diesem Fall von selbst einstellte, macht Raymond auf

ments, and at the end of the day the decisive ones, are incorporated during the painting process. Raymond finds the starting point for his motifs in the "obvious," as he calls it. This means that he draws on scenarios found in his immediate environment. These can be studio scenes, the view from a window, or arrangements in the studio resembling still-lifes. Raymond also used such an "experimental set-up" as a basis for *Electrick*. However he also emphasises the fact that he is not so much interested in the settings or objects themselves – in as much as these could just as well be different ones. He takes what is there and what seems appropriate for his visual imagery, and that is practically everything he finds in the place where he happens to be. This is usually his studio: "I let myself be inspired by everyday things," he says, "that is sometimes the sofa, tapestries, cushions and suchlike, things that are simply there. These things form a kind of fundus. It is like this: I come in, into what is in reality an arbitrary room. I presume that I am going to spend four to six hours there. During this period of time, something will happen. One can suppose that. It is like when one looks out of the window the whole time. One will see things that are completely absurd."

Raymond's settings often develop of their own accord. One example of this is the photograph that served as the template for *Orakel* (2008) [fig. p. 29] and that resulted from a very special scenario. In this picture, the spatial setting is characterised by layers: The reflection of the window blends in with the fireworks, the night sky, the camera flash and the studio wall, merging to form a dark, light-flooded interior and exterior that cannot be clearly differentiated. "I originally wanted to paint something completely different," Raymond says, "I just had this vague idea of two opposites interlocking. Then the fireworks suddenly began and they immediately became my theme. I turned the light off and was fascinated by the way in which everything was reflected in the studio. I had never seen anything like it. My visual imagery often develops this way." In this case, Raymond took something that materialized quasi by itself and made it into a process. "I draw

andere Weise dann auch zur Methode. „Ich greife den mich umgebenden Fundus an Realitäten auf, wenn ich den Eindruck habe, das könnte irgendwie Sinn ergeben. Formal, inhaltlich oder beides. In diesem Sinn sind meine Bilder eigentlich Collagen", sagt er. Im collagierenden, die Bildelemente verschmelzenden und überblendenden Malprozess kommt es ihm vor allem darauf an, was sich zeigt, wenn das Gegebene in neue, überraschende Verknüpfungen gerät und bestimmte Momente von Koinzidenz und Spannung zur Anschauung bringt. Auch wenn Raymond seine Malerei neuerdings teils sogar noch stärker ins Detail treibt, spezifische Oberflächen wie zum Beispiel Faltenwürfe erarbeitet oder Materialien wie Fell, Glas, Leder imitiert – es geht ihm niemals bloß um veristische Wiedergabe des Gegebenen. Im malerisch gebundenen Blick auf die Dinge interessiert ihn „das Naheliegende" ausdrücklich „als das Unwahrscheinliche", das er vom Vertrauten her sichtbar machen will. Solche Koinzidenzen des Unwägbaren oder sogar Irrationalen formuliert Raymond in vielen seiner Werke, sei es in der visuellen Auflösung von Raum wie in Orakel, die sich ganz dem Augenblick verdankt, oder ganz bewusst durch Konstruktion („Collage") des Imaginären wie beim schon genannten Electrick: Dort taucht in der Fensterreflexion ein Bild auf, das die Wiederholung des Gegebenen in manchen Teilen unterläuft. Im Spiegel sieht man eine schemenhafte, zentral gesetzte weibliche Figur, die an entsprechender Stelle auf dem Sofa jedoch fehlt. Sie ist als Abwesende ins Bild gerückt. Also in gewisser Weise dennoch da: Vielleicht existiert sie als Erinnerung, als Sehnsucht oder Halluzination? Sie gehört auf diese Weise untrennbar auch zur Realität des Bildes. Und steht exemplarisch für jene Art von Wahrheit, an die Raymonds Werke rühren wollen: „Letztlich geht es mir ums Durchspielen der Frage: Was ist Realität. Gibt es sie tatsächlich, oder ist es nur eine Vorstellung, die wir uns von ihr machen? Besteht da überhaupt eine Trennschärfe, und wo liegt die?" So thematisiert er das Bild als eine Schnittstelle zum Imaginären. Das, was er als Maler ohnehin betreibt – ein Verschmelzen verschiedener Wahrnehmungsschichten zwischen Vorstellung und Wirklich-

from the fundus of realities surrounding me whenever I have the feeling that it could make sense in some way. Formally, in terms of content, or both. In this sense, my pictures are in fact collages," he says. In the collaging process of painting in which the visual elements merge and are superimposed, the most important factor is what emerges when what already exists makes surprising connections, revealing specific moments of coincidence and tension. Although Raymond has recently begun to incorporate more detail into his paintings, working for example on specific surfaces such as drapes, or imitating materials such as fur, glass or leather – he is never merely concerned with the veristic reproduction of that which already exists. Viewing things in the context of painting, he is expressly interested in "the obvious" in the sense of "the improbable," which he attempts to make perceptible based on the familiar. Raymond expresses such coincidences of the imponderable or even the irrational in many of his works, whether it is the visual dissolution of space in Orakel, which can be attributed absolutely to the moment, or very consciously via the construction ("collage") of the imaginary such as in the case of the afore-mentioned work Electrick: In this case, an image appears in the reflection in the window that in part undermines the repetition of what already exists. In the mirror one sees a shadowy female figure of a woman in the centre of the picture, who is however missing from the appropriate place on the sofa. She has slipped into the picture as someone absent. Thus to some extent she is there nonetheless: Perhaps she exists as a recollection, a longing, or a hallucination? In this way she is also an inseparable part of the reality of the picture. And in an exemplary manner she represents just this kind of truth that Raymond's works strive to touch upon: "At the end of the day I am more interested in simulating the question: what is reality? Does it really exist or is it just the way we imagine reality to be? Is there a clear dividing line at all and where is it?" Thus for Raymond the picture becomes the interface with the imaginary. In paintings such as these he then causes that which he already practices as a painter – the

keit – macht er in Bildern wie diesen dann auch selbst zum Teil der Darstellung.

Das verbindet sich durchaus mit Ironie und einer gewissen Spielfreude, wenn Raymond gelegentlich ganz unterschiedliche Bilder motivisch durch winzige Details wie in einem Suchspiel miteinander verknüpft: Das pelzige Etwas aus dem kleinen Reineke (2008) [Abb. S. 33], dort mit Lampen oder so etwas wie absurden Augen ausgestattet, findet sich auch im großformatigen Ponton (2008) [Abb. S. 31], dort am Rand des Geländers platziert. Oder wird in Neuro (2007) [Abb. S. 19] in geradezu altmeisterlicher Darstellung präsentiert. „Ich möchte mit solchen Gesten einen Zusammenhang schaffen", so Raymond, „der die Bilder wie ein ,character' oder ein Logo verbindet." Dadurch lässt er zwischen einzelnen Bildern teils regelrecht spukhafte Verknüpfungen auftauchen, etwa durch die kleinen, intensiv rot glimmenden Punkte, die die ansonsten so grundverschiedenen Arbeiten wie das lapidare, bühnenhafte Stecken (2007) [Abb. S. 26] und den industrieromantischen Fernblick in Weinsberger Kreuz (2007) [Abb. S. 27] verbinden. Im skizzenhaften Bild Sessel (2007) [Abb. S. 53] verleiht Raymond diesen kleinen, bohrend blickenden Spots dann doch noch ein Gesicht, und zwar ausdrücklich auch ein geisterhaftes. Im Ganzen bleiben sie vor allem rätselhaft, Platzhalter eines ungesehenen Schauens, mit dem in Raymonds Bilderwelt die Wirklichkeit durchsetzt ist und ihr eine Schicht des Unwirklichen hinzufügen.

Das Bild als Schnittstelle zum Imaginären – das gilt auf andere Weise ebenso für Weiher (2008) (zu dem übrigens auch eine kleine, das Motiv vorbereitende Ölskizze Stift (2007) existiert [Abb. S. 2]. Man sieht eine idyllische Landschaft, ein See, der das Umgebungsgrün so spiegelt, dass darin Bild und Abbildrealität verschwimmen beziehungsweise gleichgewichtig gegeneinander geführt sind: Die Uferlinie auf Mittelachse markiert die horizontale Grenze zwischen Wasser und Land, und ein zentral gesetzter Baum verlängert sich gespiegelt in der Vertikalen abwärts. Beides zusammen fügt sich zum womöglich auch sakral zu deutenden Bildgeviert. Mit Mitteln der Malerei stellt Raymond hier die Frage nach dem Bildraum und seinem

merging of different layers of awareness between perception and reality – to become part of the depiction itself.

It is not without a certain amount of pleasure taken in playfulness and a touch of irony that Raymond sometimes links motifs in very different pictures by means of minute details, like in a game of hide and seek: the furry something in the small work Reineke (2008) [fig. p. 33], present in this work with lamps or absurd-looking eyes can also be found in the large format work Ponton (2008) [fig. p. 31], standing at the edge of the railing. Or it is depicted quite in the style of the Old Masters in Neuro (2007) [fig. p. 19]. "Using such gestures I aim to create a context," Raymond says, one that links the pictures like a "character" or a logo. In this way, he sometimes allows quite spooky connections to emerge, for example using the small dots with their intense red glow to link the otherwise completely different works such as the succinct, stage-like work Stecken (2007) [fig. p. 26] and the industrial-romantic view into the distance in Weinsberger Kreuz (2007) [fig. p. 27]. In the roughly sketched picture Sessel (2007) [fig. p. 53], Raymond gives these small, inquisitive-looking spotlights a face after all, in fact an explicitly ghostly one. Above all, they generally remain mysterious, placeholders for an unseen spectacle, with which reality can be enforced in Raymond's world of images and to which a layer of irreality can be added.

The picture as the interface to the world of imagination – this also applies in another way to the work Weiher (2008), which also includes a small oil painting Stift (2007), a preparatory draft for the motif [fig. p. 2]. Here one can see an idyllic landscape, a lake, that reflects the surrounding greenery in such a way that the image and the reality of the representation merge or rather serve to balance each other out: The riverbank along the central axis marks the horizontal border between the water and the land, and a centrally positioned tree extends downwards in a vertical reflection. Together, both combine to create a pictorial space that could also possibly be perceived as sacred. Using the medium of painting, Raymond questions this pictorial space and its relationship to reality: These pictures

Verhältnis zur Realität: Es gehe in diesen Bildern „eben um Kreuzung und Koinzidenz", sagt er, „ganz unmittelbar etwa in der Frage: Auf welcher Seite liegt der ‚wirkliche' Teich? Was zeigt die spiegelnde Scheibe in Electrick tatsächlich? Begriffe wie Transzendenz oder Membran spielen da eine Rolle, vielleicht sogar die Vorstellung vom Übertritt in eine andere Welt. Das ist ja immer das Thema – hier mit der Fensterscheibe, dort durch die Wasserfläche. Mir geht es darum, unserer oberflächlichen Betrachtungsweise der Realität andere Vorstellungsweisen entgegenzuhalten. Jenseits der Erklärungsmuster, wie wir sie im Allgemeinen so verwenden und nach denen wir im Alltag funktionieren. Mich interessiert, was passiert, wenn das Unterbewusste durchdringt, in bestimmten Zuständen etwa wie im Halbschlaf, in denen sich unterschiedliche Vorstellungen von Realität vermischen."

Mit derartigen Überblendungen die treffende Pointe des Befremdens am Vertrauten zu erwischen, das ist bei Raymond stets auch eine Frage von Finetuning und intuitiver Verknüpfung. In 24h (2008) [Abb. S. 22] zum Beispiel: Der Bildaufbau ist einfach, die Elemente als solche sind unschwer zu entziffern – doch im Zusammenspiel ist alles plötzlich von so verschobener Realität wie ein Traumbild kurz vor dem Erwachen. Das Bild ist stimmig, hat behauptende Kraft, und dennoch führt es Tageswirklichkeit auf bezwingend leichte Weise ad absurdum. Im Vordergrund und dominierend ragt da ein schwarzer Faltenwurf in die Höhe, massig und steil wie ein Gebirgsmassiv. Und erscheint im nächsten Augenblick auch federleicht wie eine von der Decke abgehängte Plastikplane. Dahinter erstrahlt ein kräftig blauer, klarer Himmel, der sich an anderer Stelle in neonhelle, violette Nacht verwandelt. Links unten ist ein Stückchen Wolfspelz drapiert, das kauernd wie ein kleines Tier erscheint, aber dann erkennbar doch nur leere Hülle ist – hohl wie wohl auch dieses schwarze Etwas, das sich über ihm, sei's schützend, sei's bedrohlich, ausbreitet. Man muss Bilder wie dieses nicht mit expliziten Lesarten und Deutungen befrachten, um sie zu verstehen. Es sind Spiegelbilder der Imagination, und darin ist das Leichte dem Schweren verwandt, Belebtes kann plötz-

"happen to be about hybridisation and coincidence," he says, "very directly for example when asking the question: which side is the 'real' lake on? What does the reflective disc in *Electrick* really show? Terms such as transcendence or membrane play a role here, perhaps even the concept of a passage into another world. That is always the issue – with the window here, through the water's surface there. For me it is all about countering our superficial point of view with the reality of other ways of perceiving. Beyond explanatory models such as those we generally use and according to which we function in everyday life. I am interested in what happens when the unconscious comes through, in particular situations such as the period of time between sleeping and waking, during which different perceptions of reality merge."

Capturing the essence of the unfamiliar within the familiar is for Raymond always a question of fine-tuning and intuitive connecting. In *24h* (2008) [fig. p. 22] for example: the composition of the picture is simple, the elements as such are not hard to decipher – however on interacting everything suddenly becomes displaced, there a shift in reality like a dream image shortly before awakening. The picture is coherent, and has a predicative strength, yet it still leads the reality of day ad absurdum in a compellingly light-hearted manner. Dominant in the foreground, a black drape protrudes upwards, bulky and steep like a massif. And the next moment it appears light as a feather, like one of the pieces of plastic sheeting hanging from the ceiling. Behind it there is a strong blue clear sky, which is transformed in another section into a violet-neon night. Below, on the left, a piece of wolf skin has been draped and seems to crouch like a small animal only then to become recognisable as an empty shell – hollow just like this black something stretched over it, whether it be protectively or threateningly. It is not necessary to burden the pictures with explicit interpretations or meanings. They reflect the imagination, and in them lightness is closely related to heaviness. Something enlivened can in another moment appear to be an empty shell or vice versa, while the whole picture suddenly appears like a section that is

lich als Hülle erscheinen oder umgekehrt, während das
ganze Bild auf einmal wie ein Ausschnitt wirkt, der ange-
wiesen bleibt auf Mutmaßungen über das Jenseits der
Ränder. Mit dieser Art von Präzision arbeitet Raymond am
offenen Bild.

Das gelingt ihm auf andere Weise und in feiner Andeu-

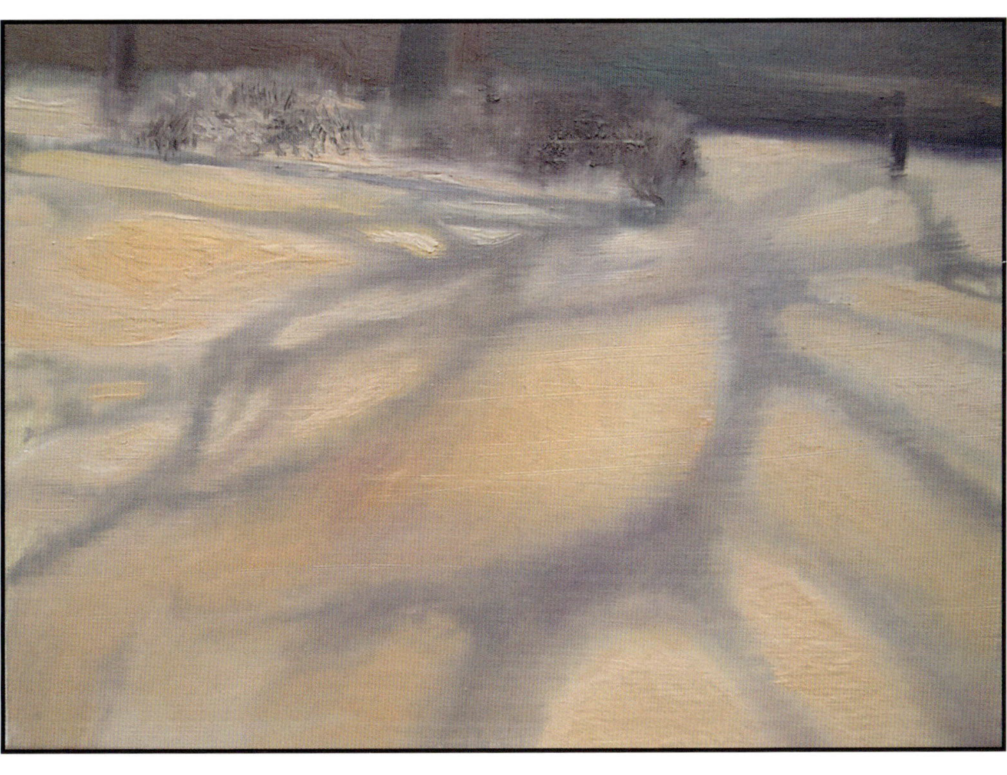

tung auch mit kleinen Formaten, die vergleichsweise un-
spektakulär erscheinen mögen, auf vielleicht stillere Art
aber ebenfalls aufs „Unwahrscheinliche" hin ausgerichtet
sind. Neuschnee (2006) [Abb. S. 15] ist zum Beispiel so
eine in Malerei gefasste Augenblicksaufnahme, die den
‚decisive moment', in dem Erscheinung zum Bild wird,
unmittelbar im Wirklichen entdeckt und festhält. Das kleine Stück Winterlandschaft ist nach oben durch einen sch-
malen, nach rechts leicht abwärts gekippten Streifen in
Braungrün begrenzt, der genauso gut Himmel sein könnte wie eine Scheunenwand: Eben etwas, das den Horizont,
sei's materiell, sei's immateriell, begrenzt. Davor zwei
Stämme, vom Bildrand stark beschnitten, und etwas kah-

les Buschwerk. All das hält Raymond knapp und skizzenhaft. Der mit Abstand größte Teil des Bildes zeigt eine Fläche frisch gefallenen Schnees, der sich wie unberührte Leinwand ausbreitet und damit eine Folie bildet für das Spiel von seltsam orangefarbenem Licht und den blaugrauen Schatten unbelaubter Äste. Was Raymond hier zur Darstellung bringt, grenzt ans „Fast Nichts" und macht die leere, kalte Landschaft zur Bühne eines immateriellen Ineinanders aus warmfarbigem Licht und ausgreifenden Schatten, die beinahe wie Adern oder Arme wirken. Es ist eine augenblickshafte Koinzidenz und ein beiläufiger Moment von befremdender Schönheit. Neuschnee führt in skizzenhafter, atmosphärisch dichter Leichtigkeit vor Augen, was charakteristisch ist für Raymonds Malerei im Ganzen: Das Unwahrscheinliche ist eine besondere Art, das Wirkliche zu sehen.

Jens Asthoff

that is characteristic of Raymond's painting on the whole: Improbability is a special way of perceiving reality.

Jens Asthoff
(Translation: Gillian Morris)

1 Alle Zitate: Alexander Raymond im Gespräch mit dem Autor am 22.10. 2008 in Raymonds Atelier in Hamburg.

1 All quotes: Alexander Raymond in conversation with the author on 22.10. 2008 in Raymond's studio in Hamburg.

Abbildungen | Plates

Neuro
2007
30 x 40 cm

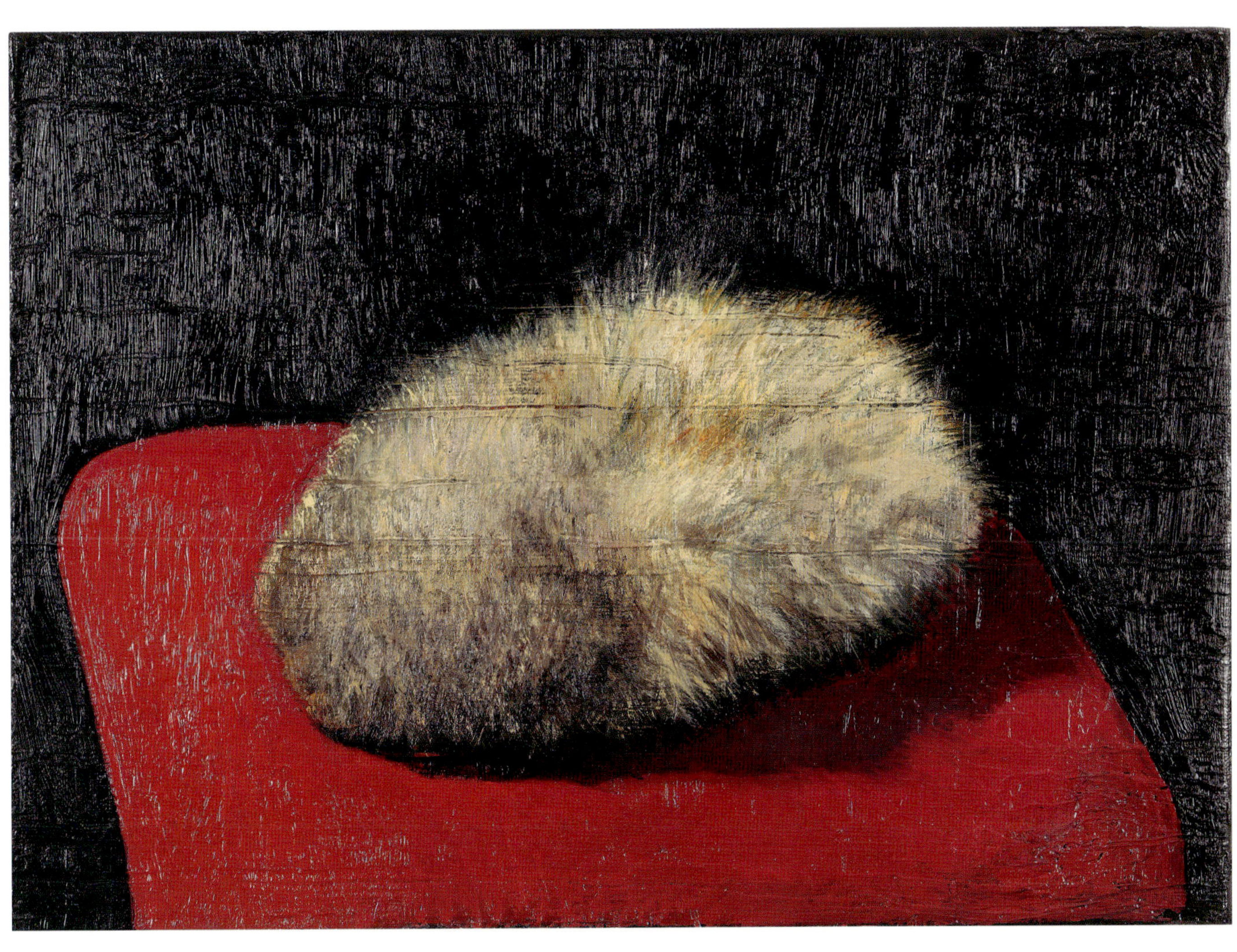

Flamme
2007
120 x 140 cm

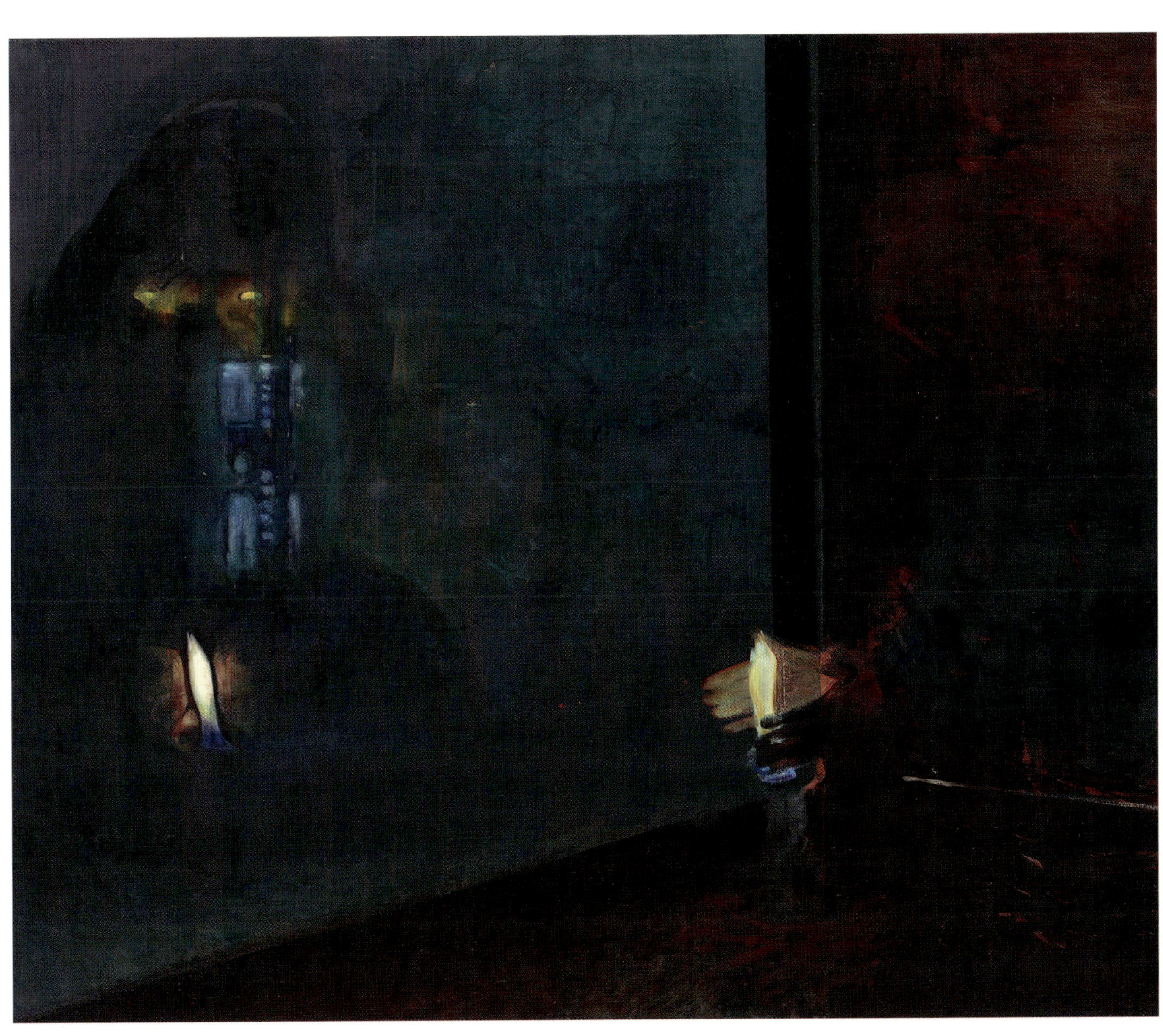

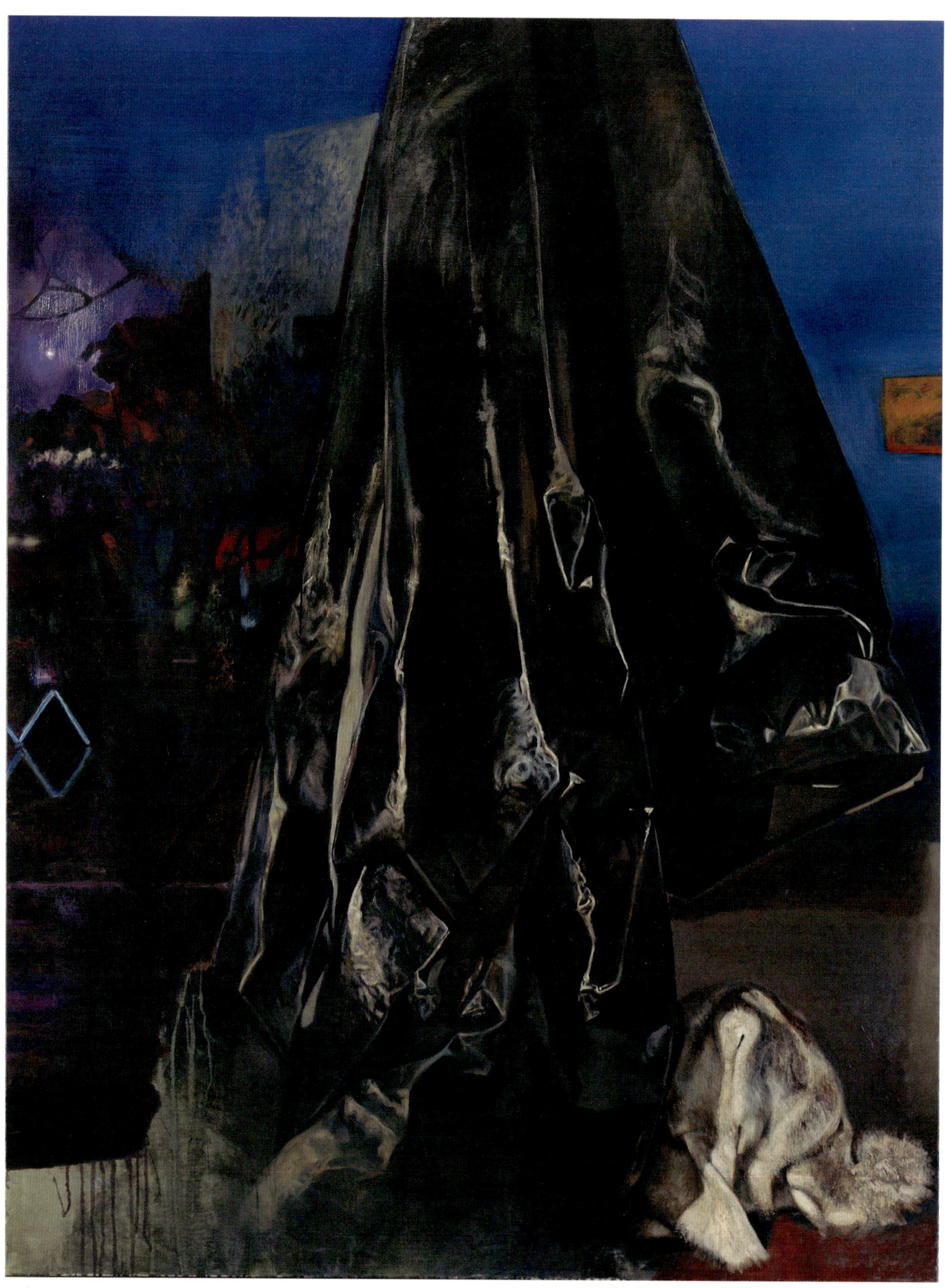

24h
2008
190 x 140 cm

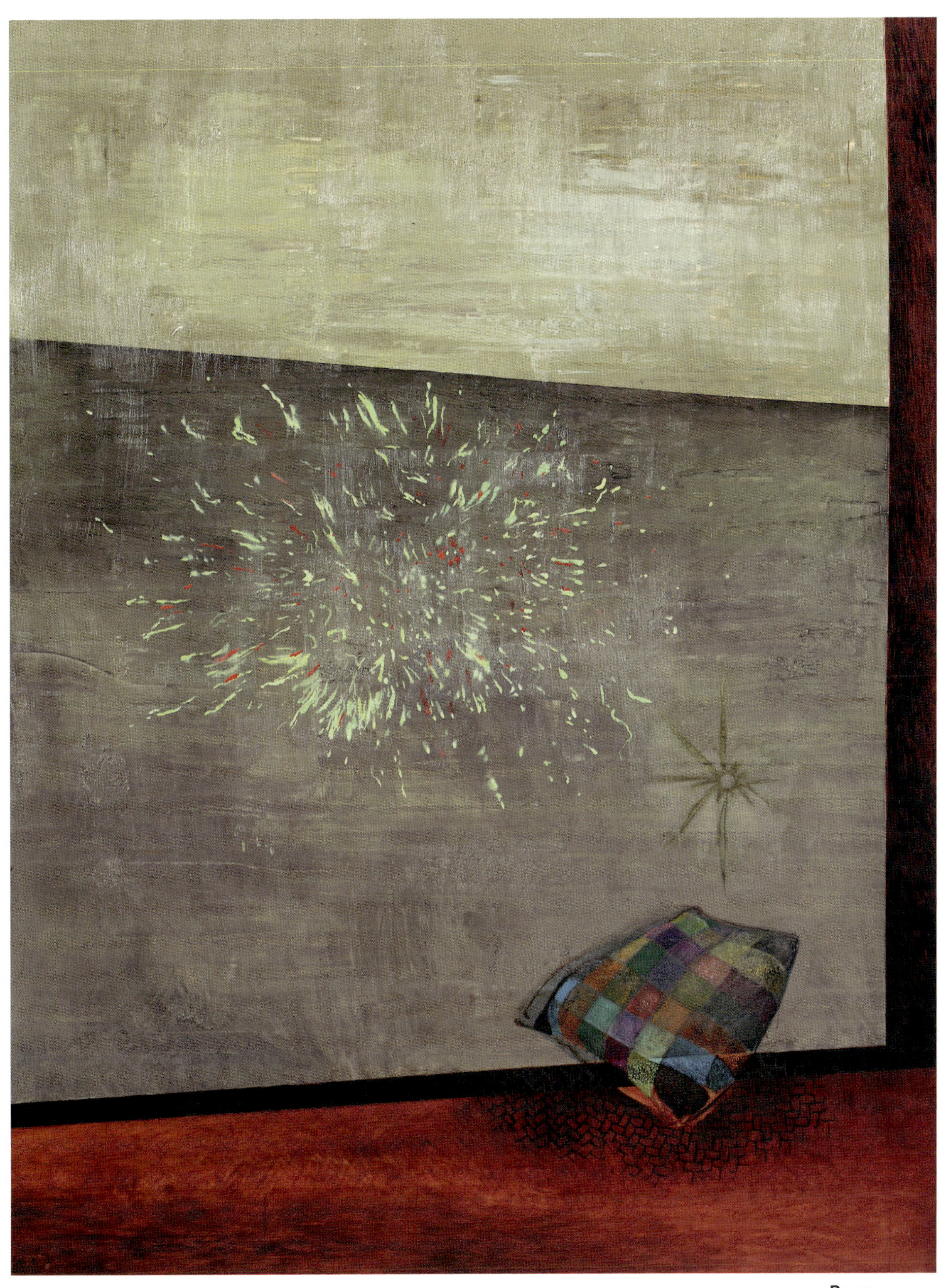

Bang
2008
190 x 140 cm

Abnoe
2007
110 x 190 cm

24

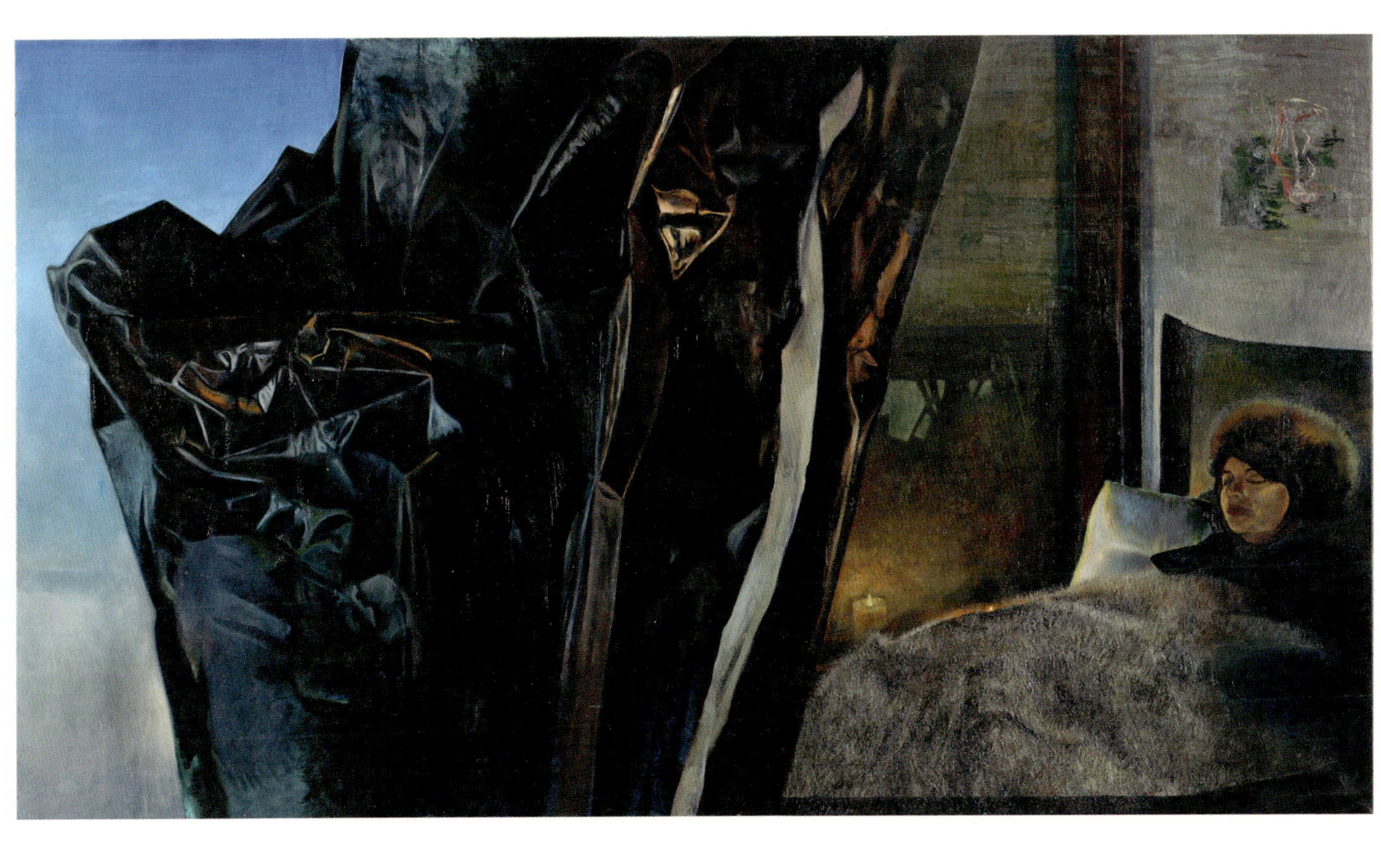

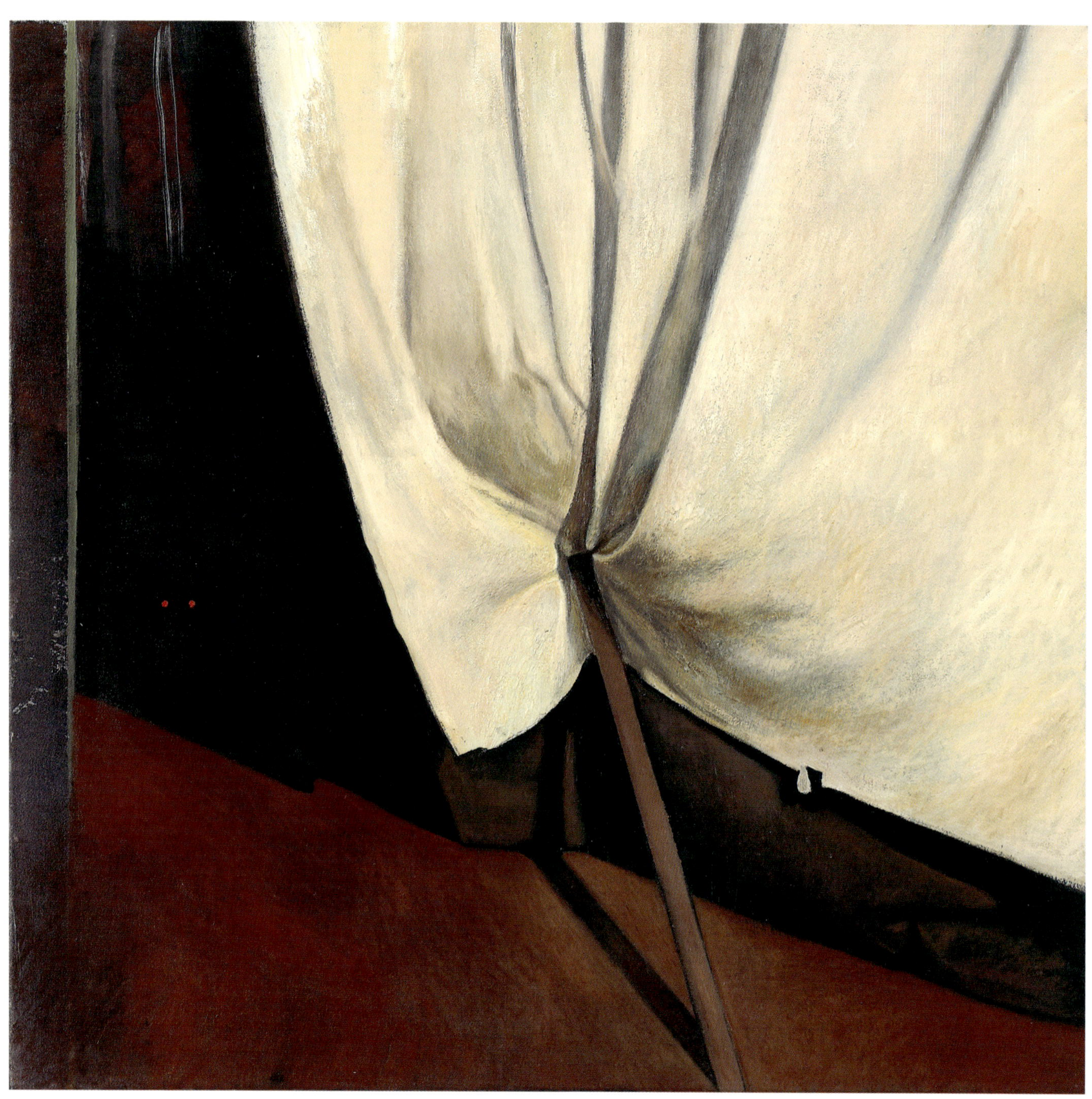

Stecken
2007
90 x 90 cm

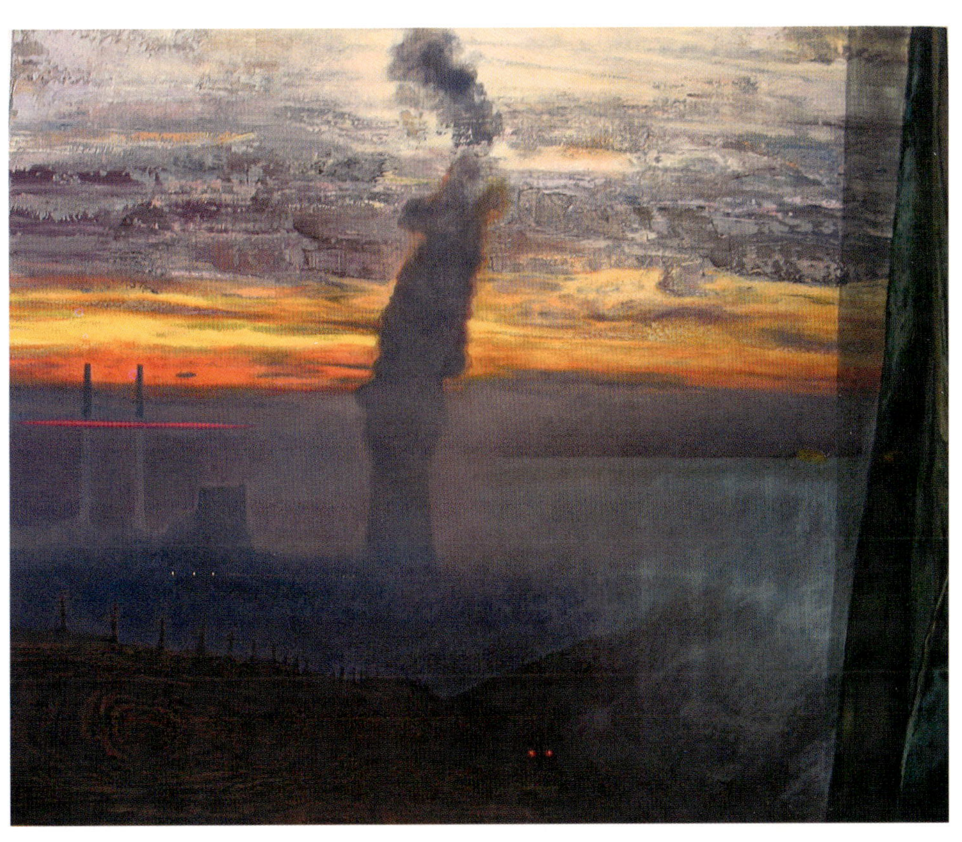

Weinsberger Kreuz
2007
120 x 140 cm

Orakel
2008
120 x 140 cm

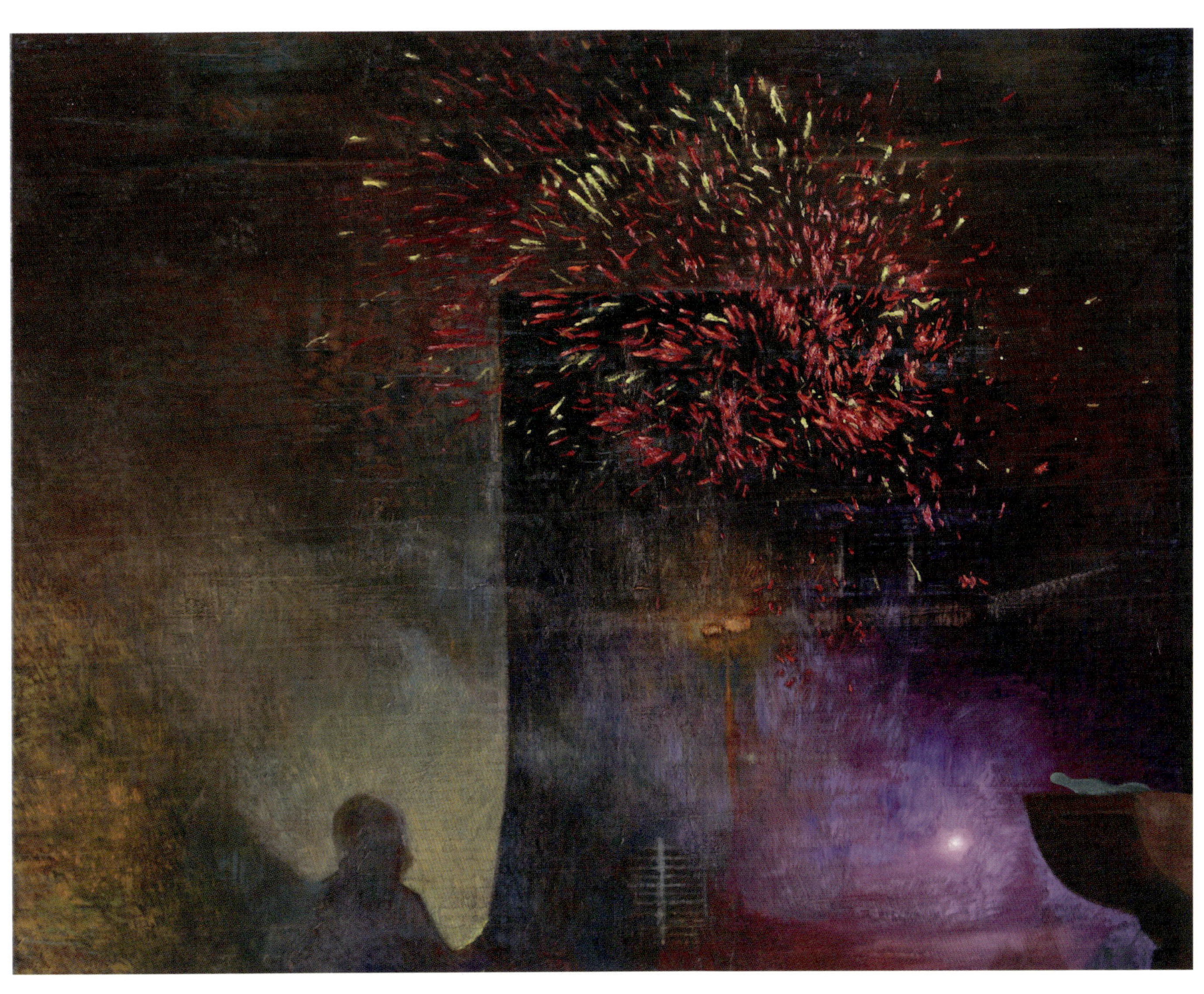

Ponton
2008
210 x 160 cm

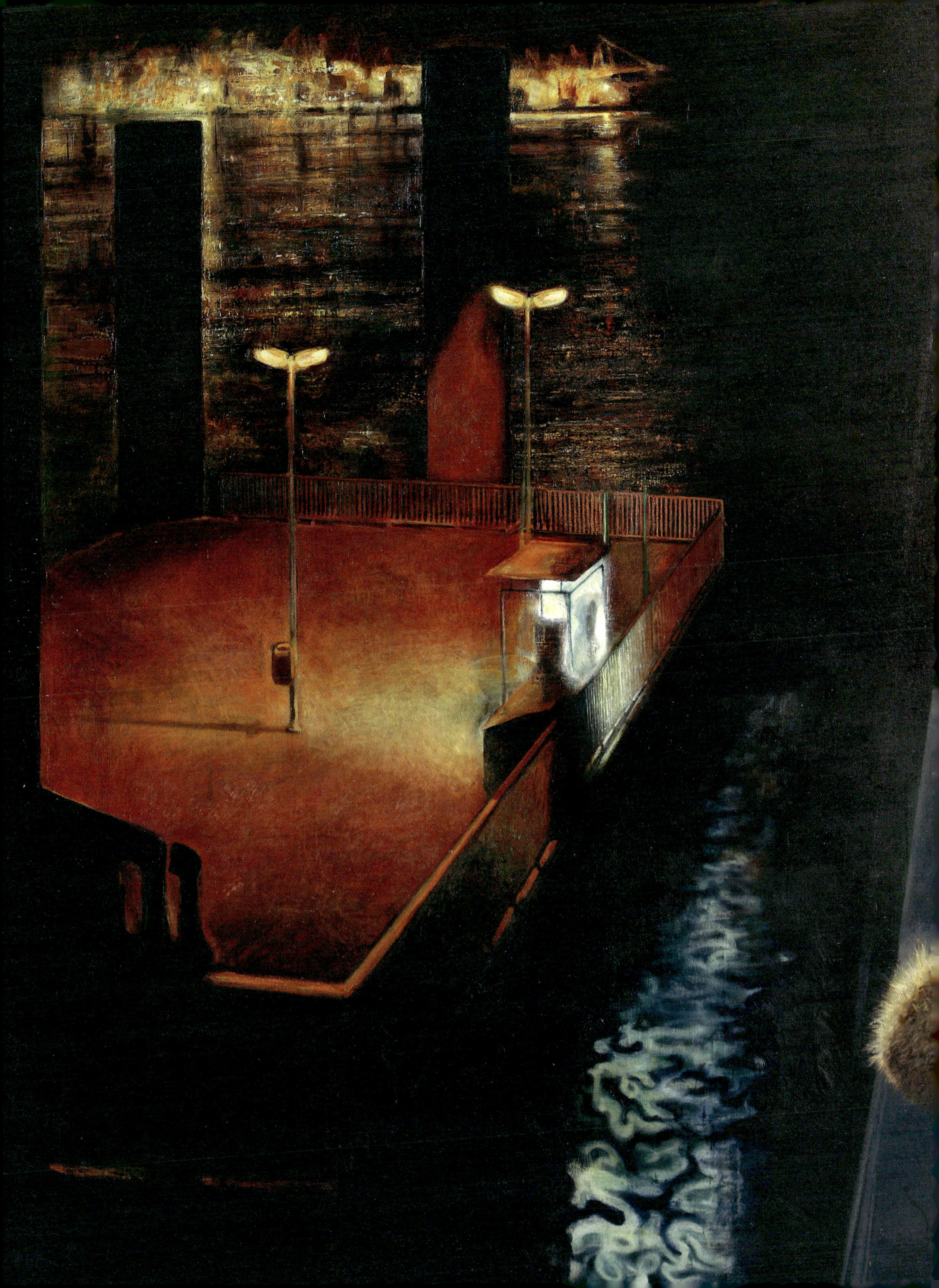

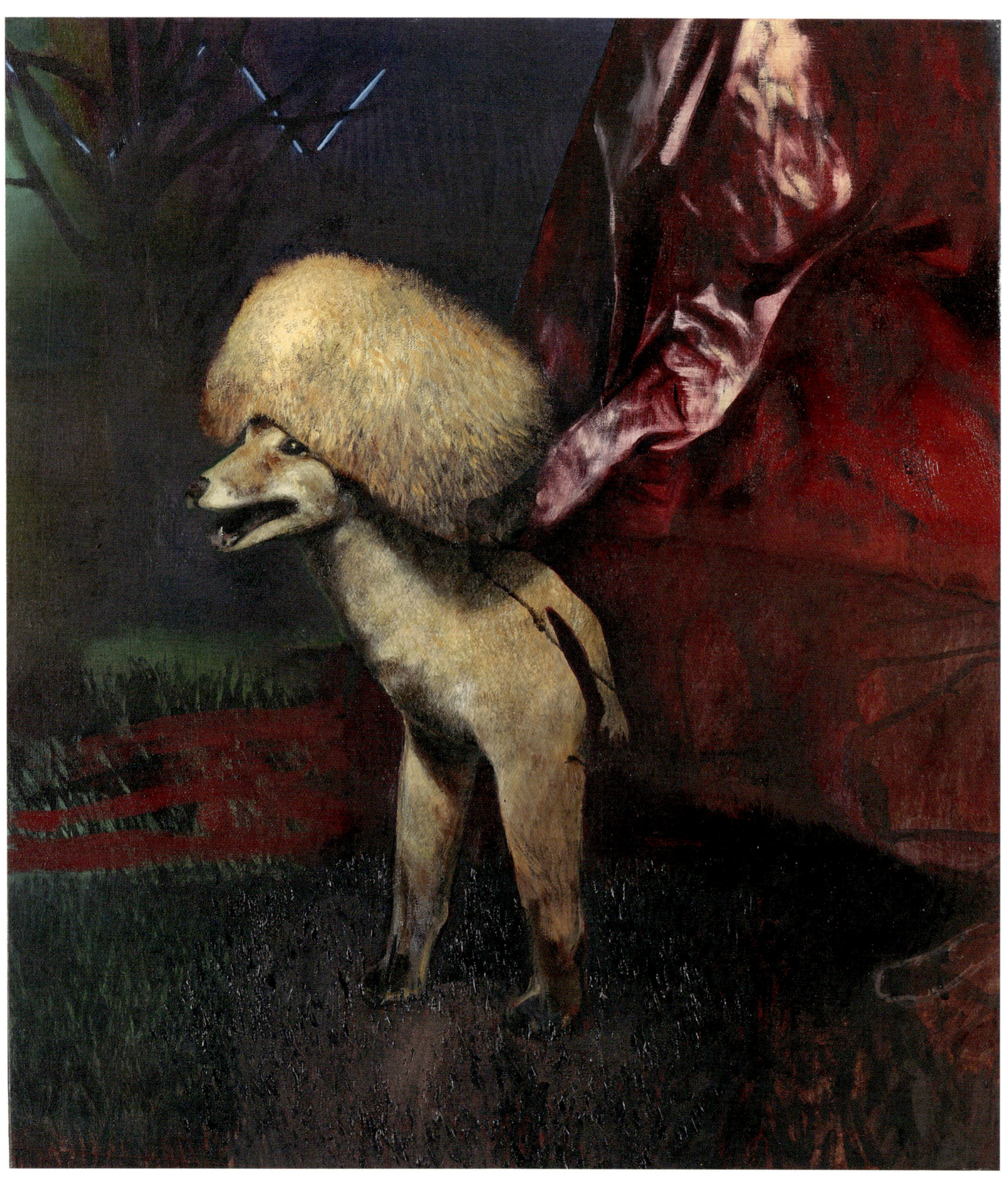

Fux
2008
70 x 60 cm

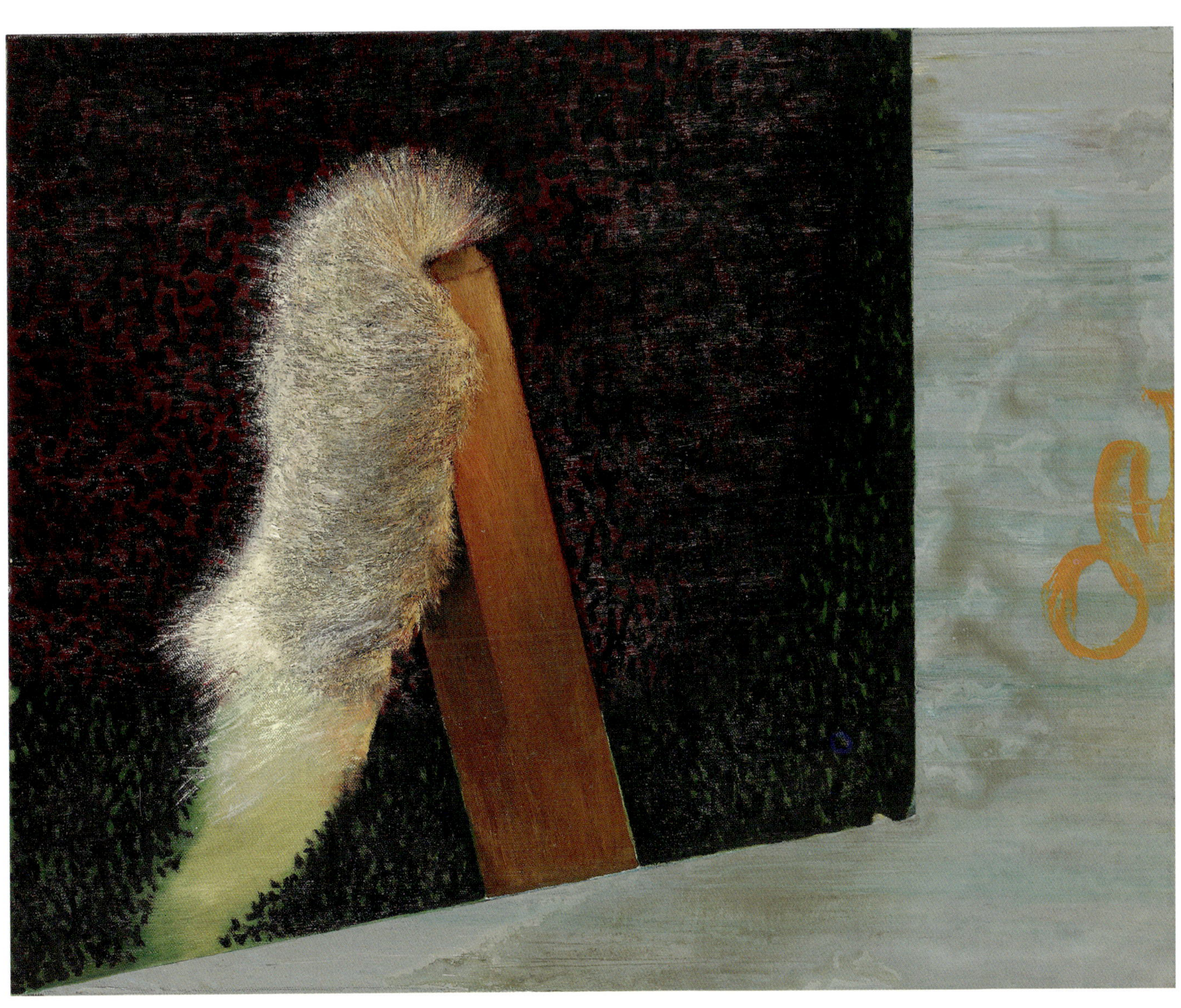

Pank
2008
60 x 50 cm

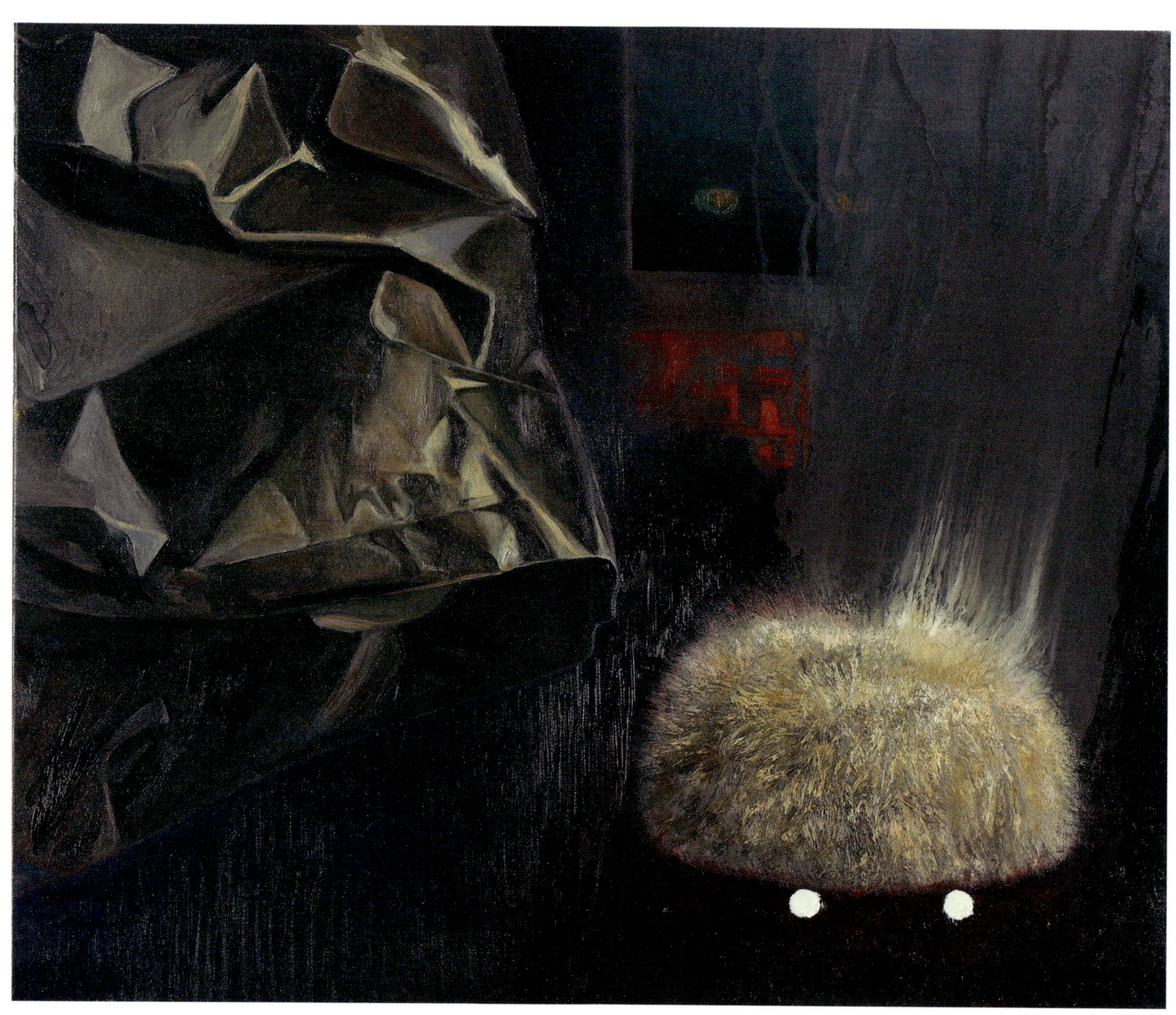

Reineke
2008
60 x 70 cm

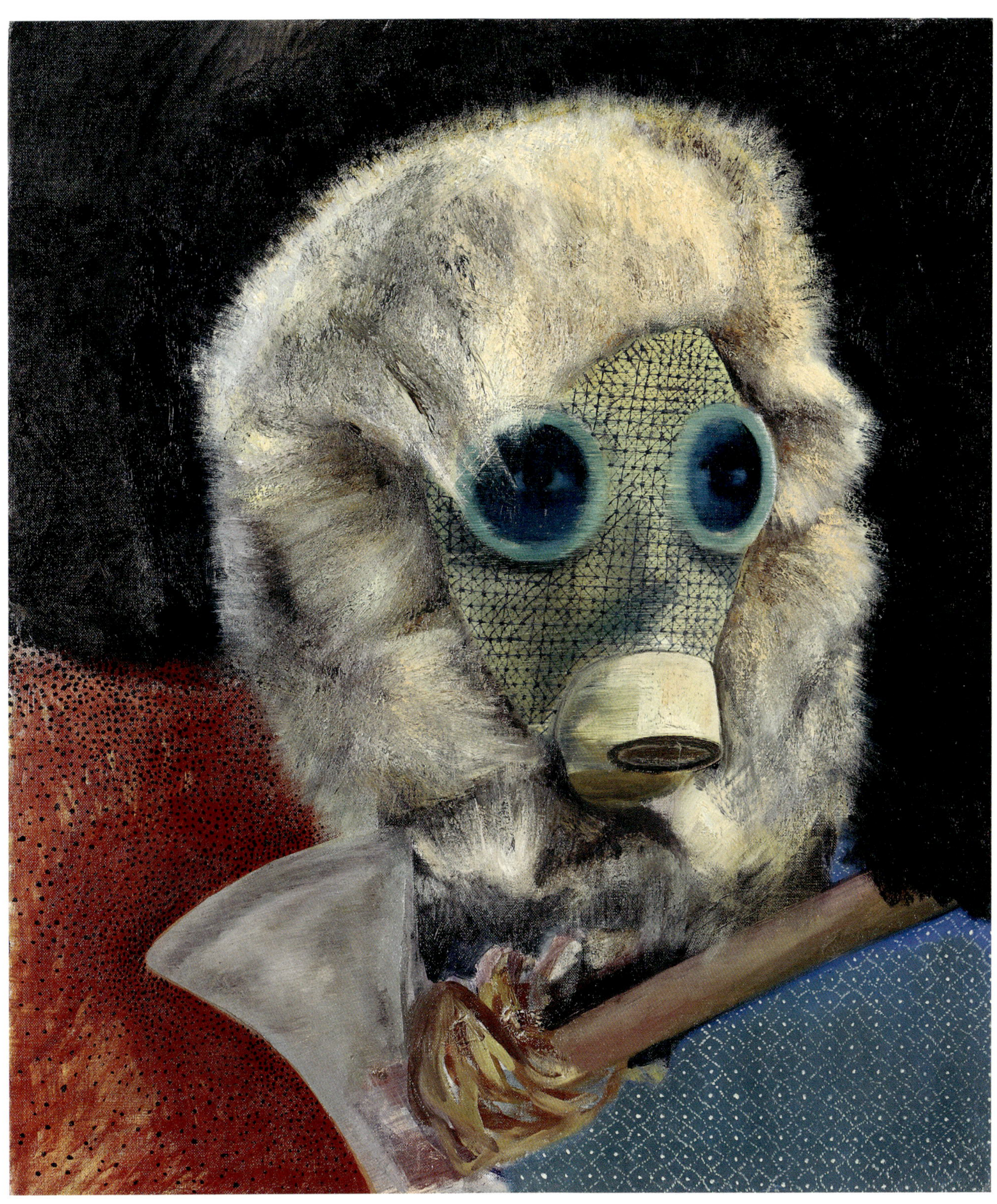

Maske

2007

60 x 50 cm

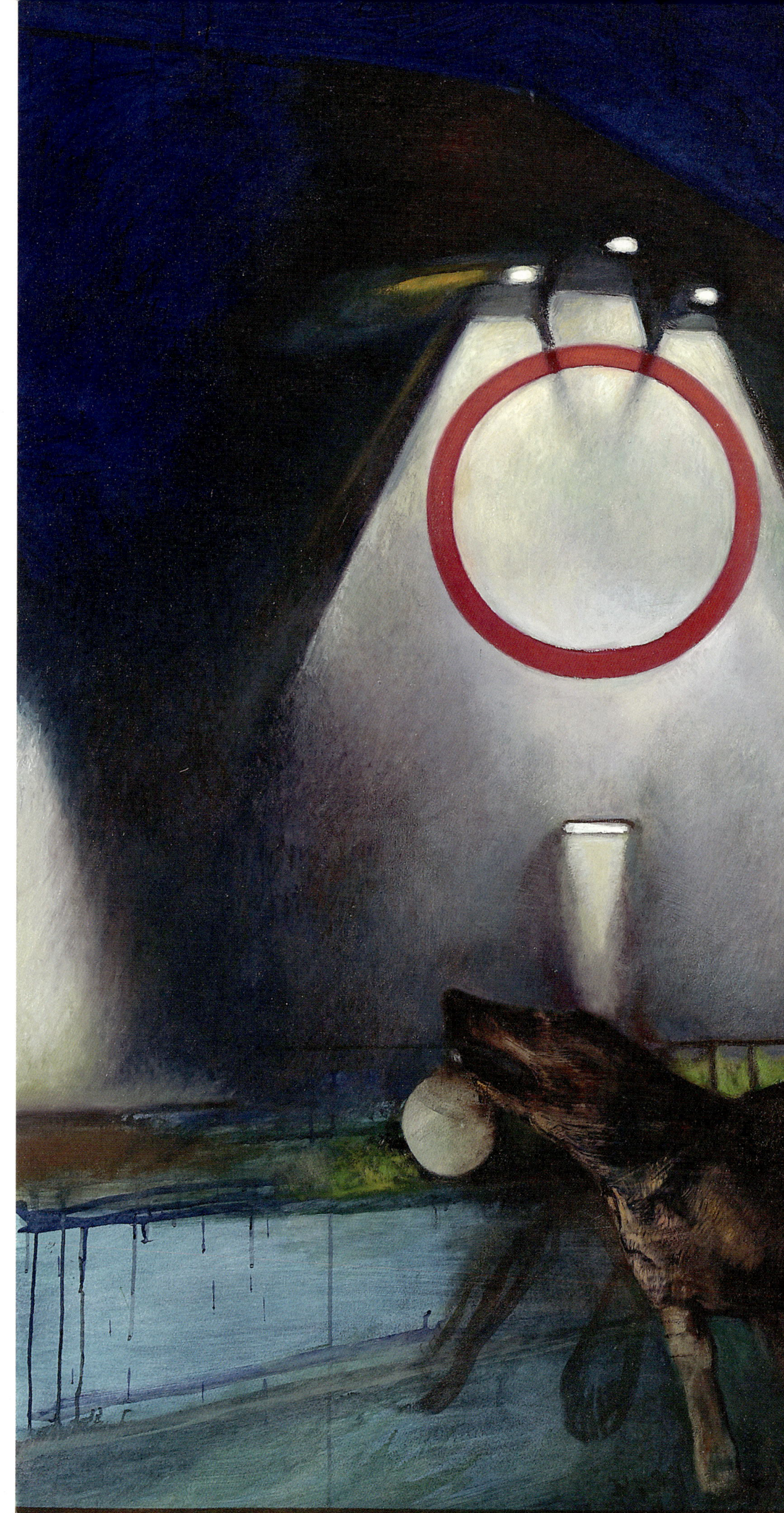

Kreis
2008
165 x 210 cm

36

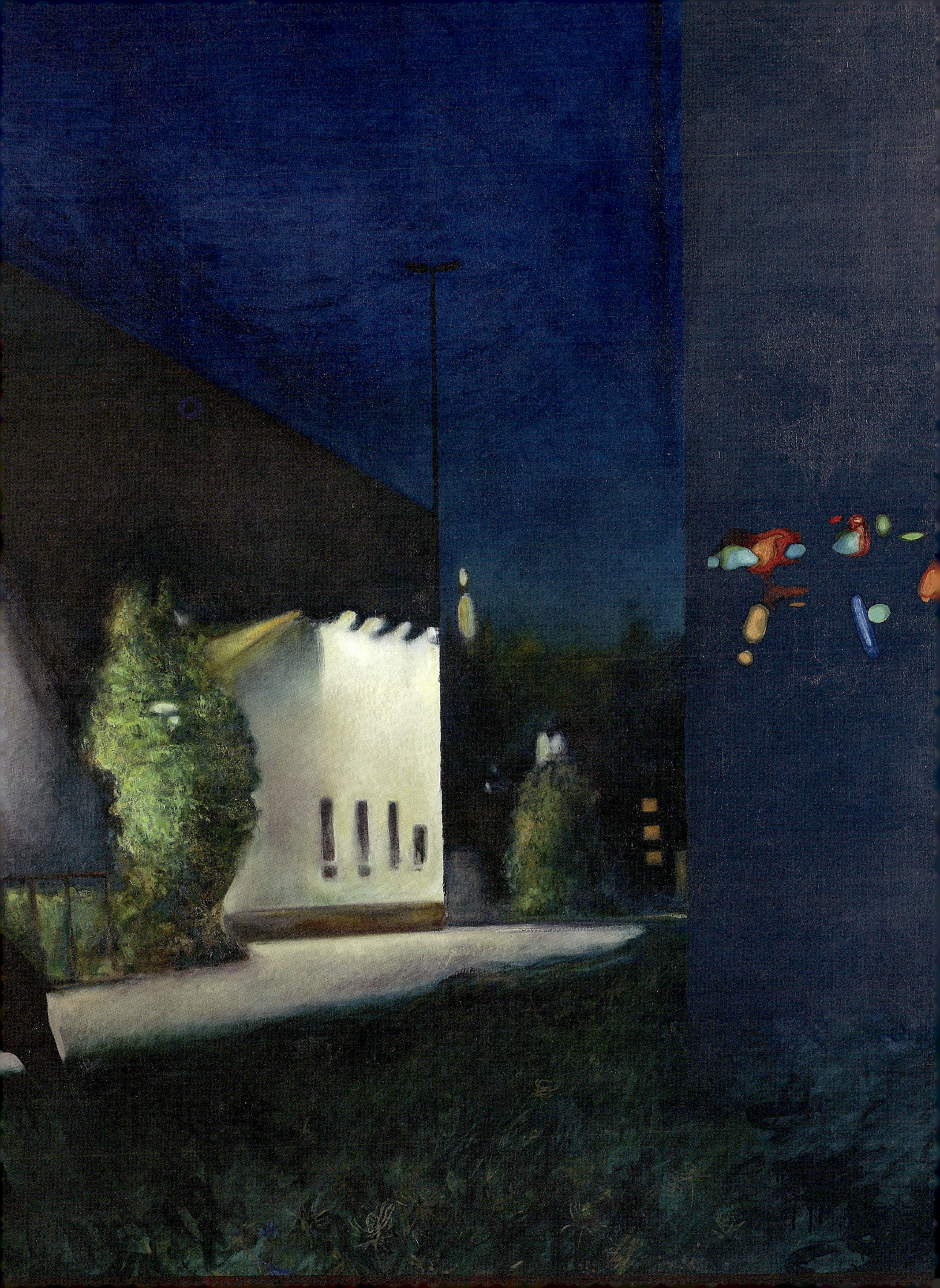

Perro
2008
90 x 100 cm

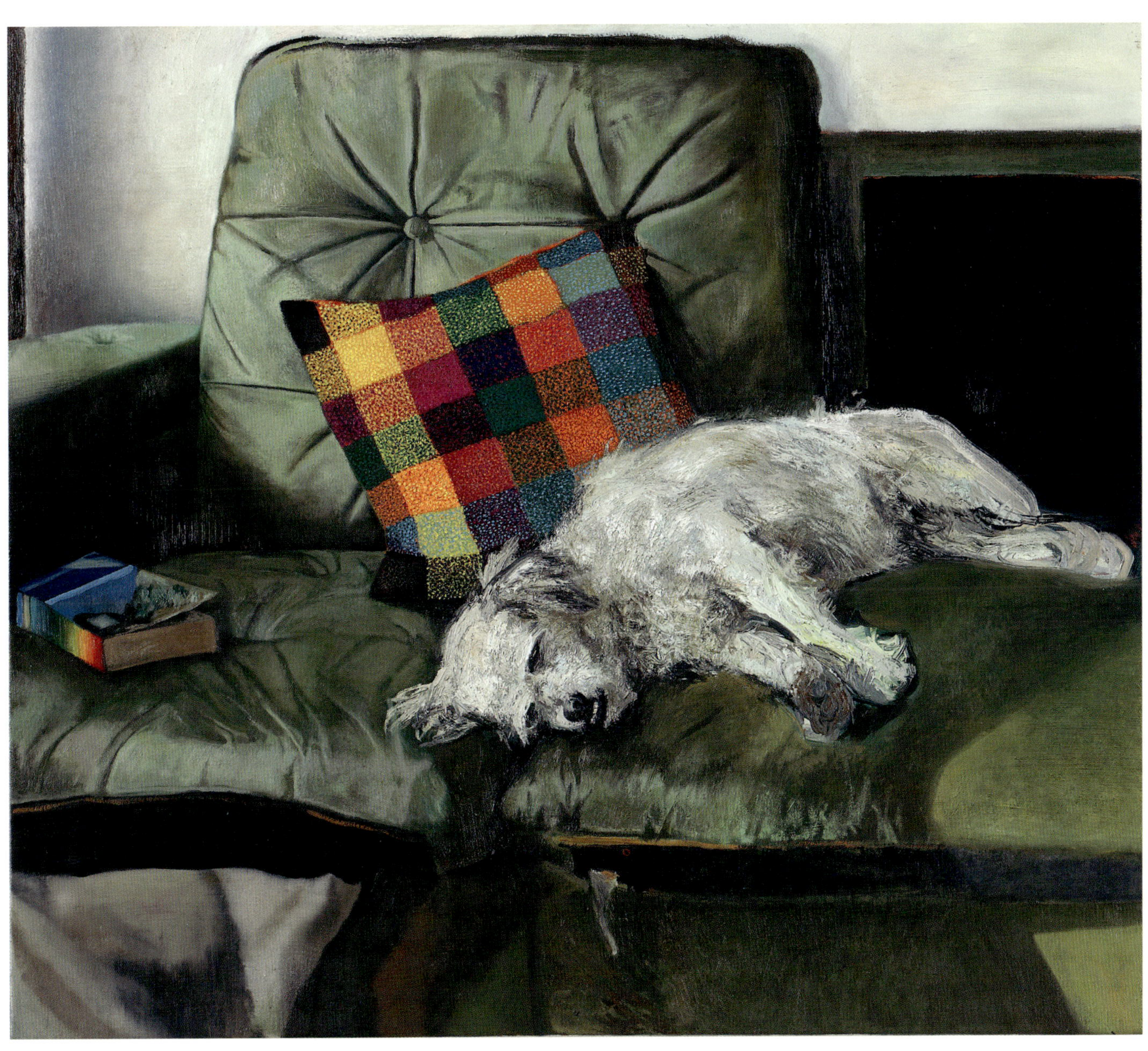

Ozeanien
2008
90 x 100 cm

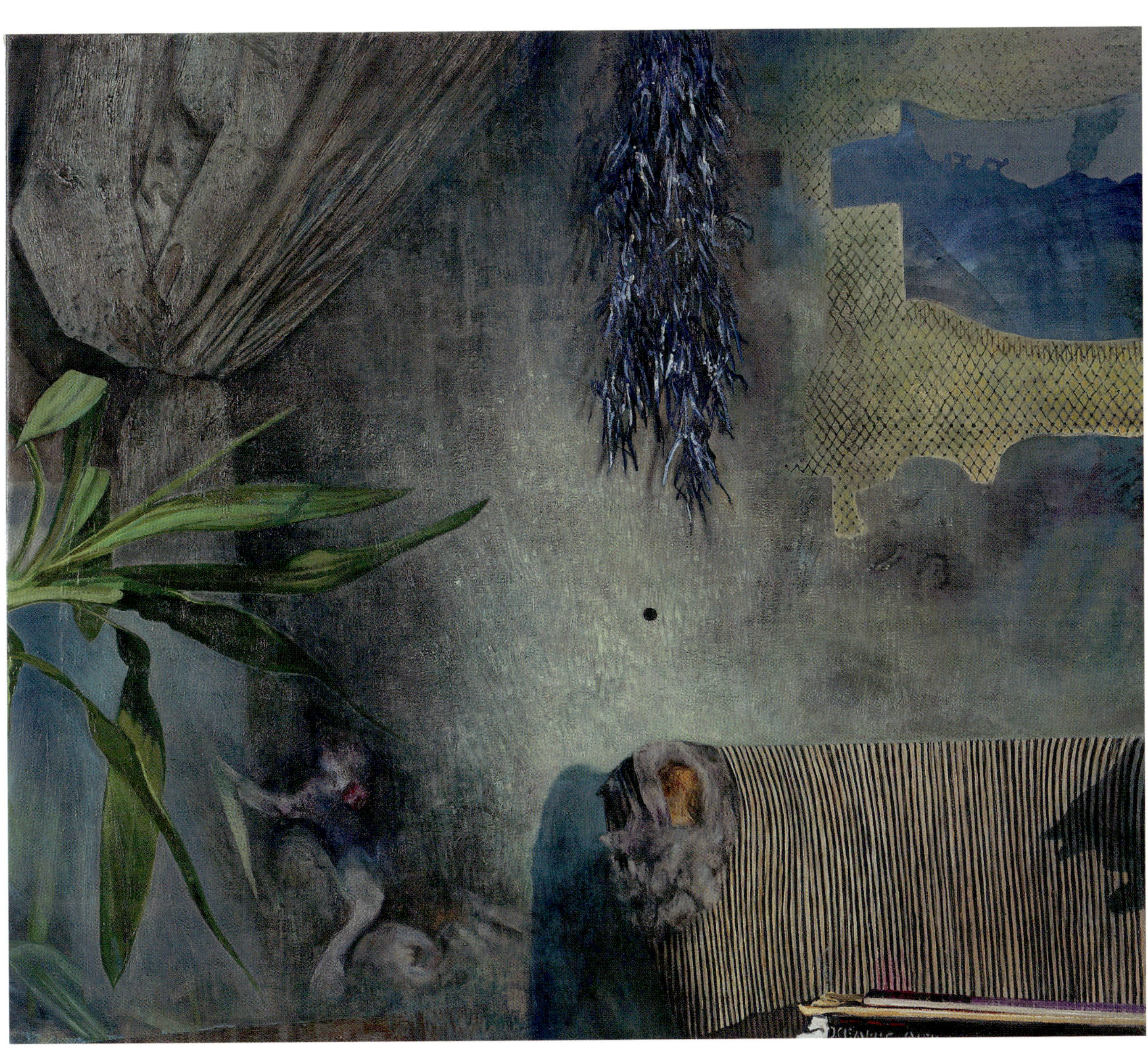

G.
2008
100 x 90 cm

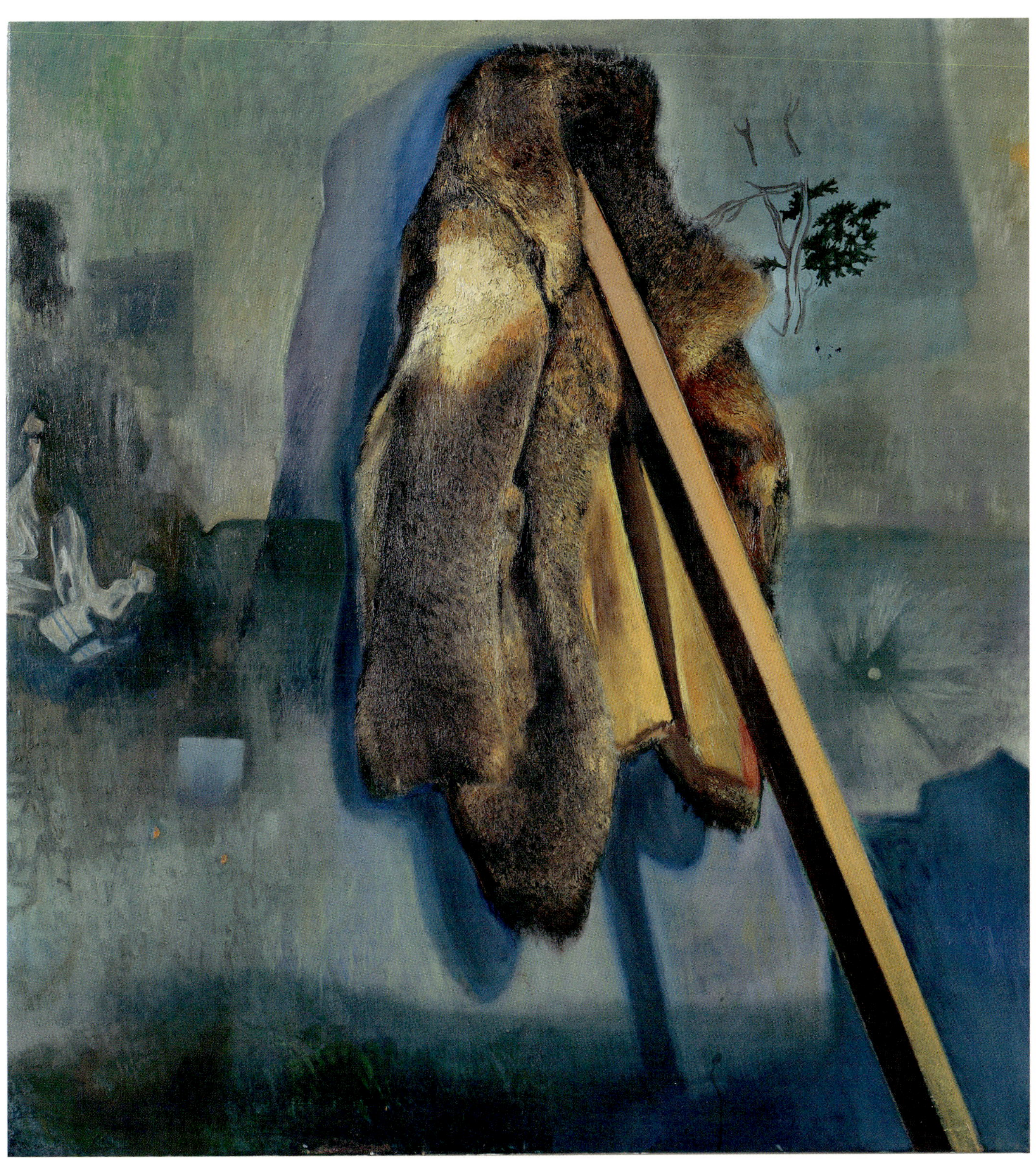

Eco
2007
90 x 100 cm

44

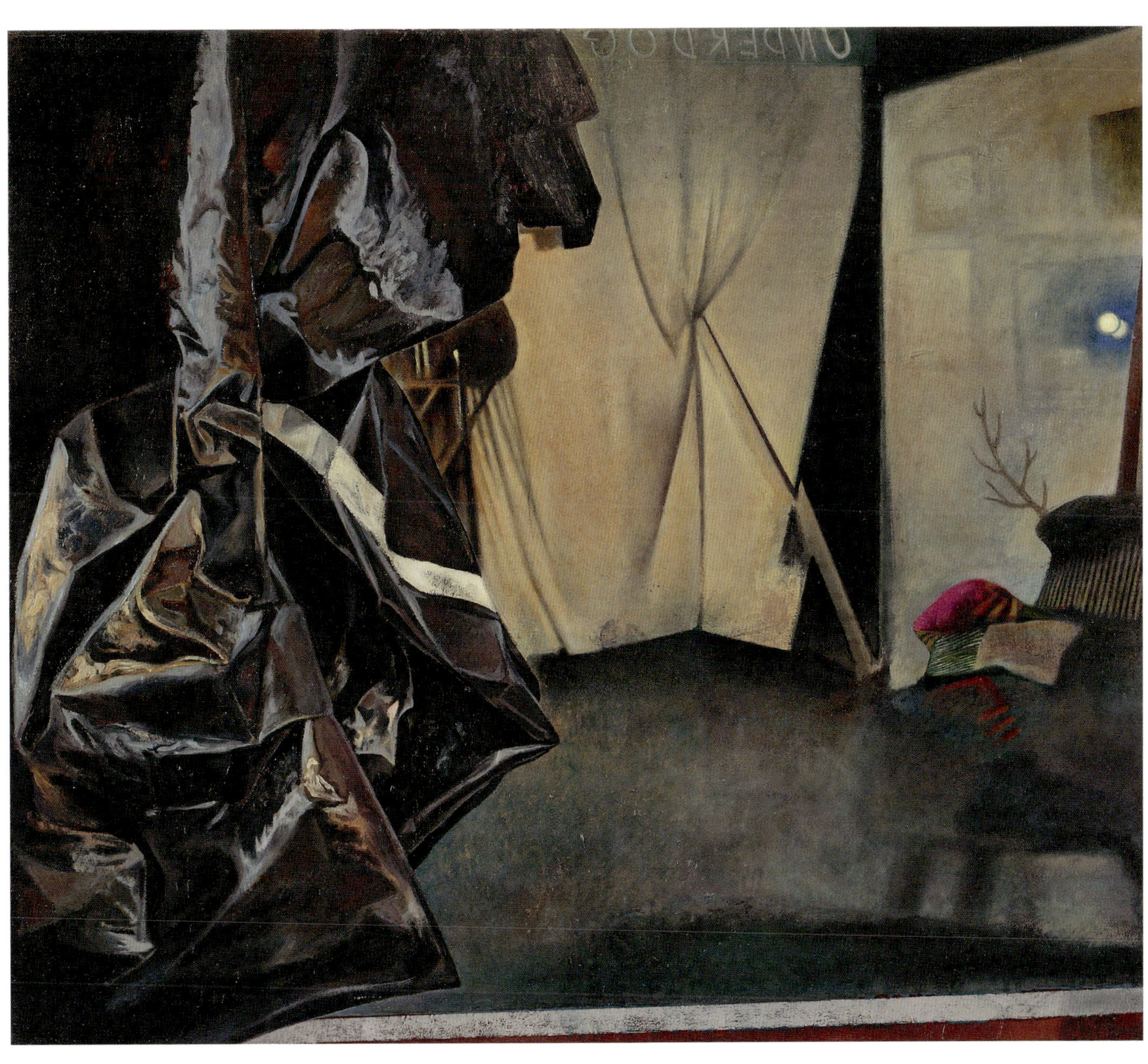

Flasche
2008
80 x 100 cm

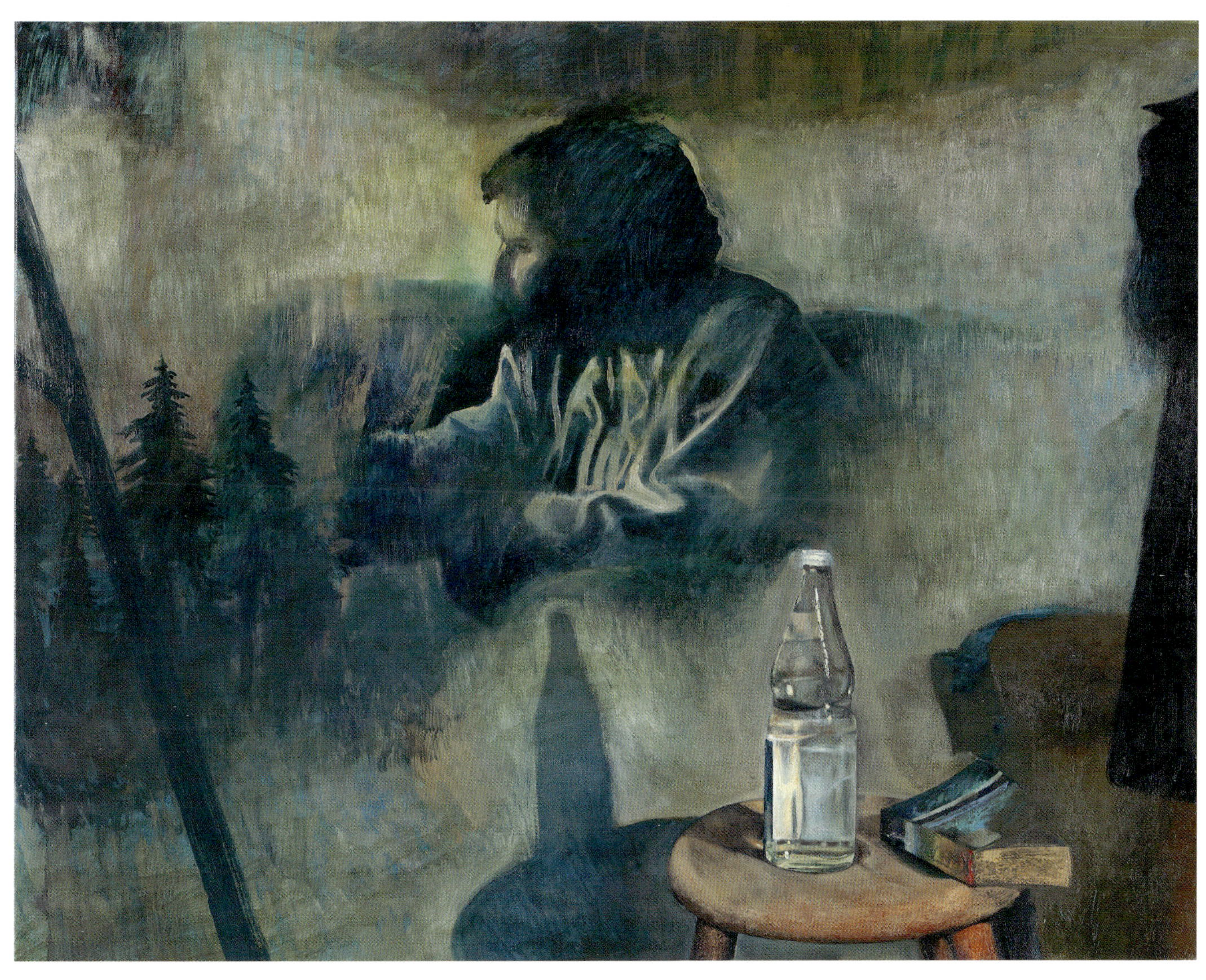

Electrick
2008
200 x 175 cm

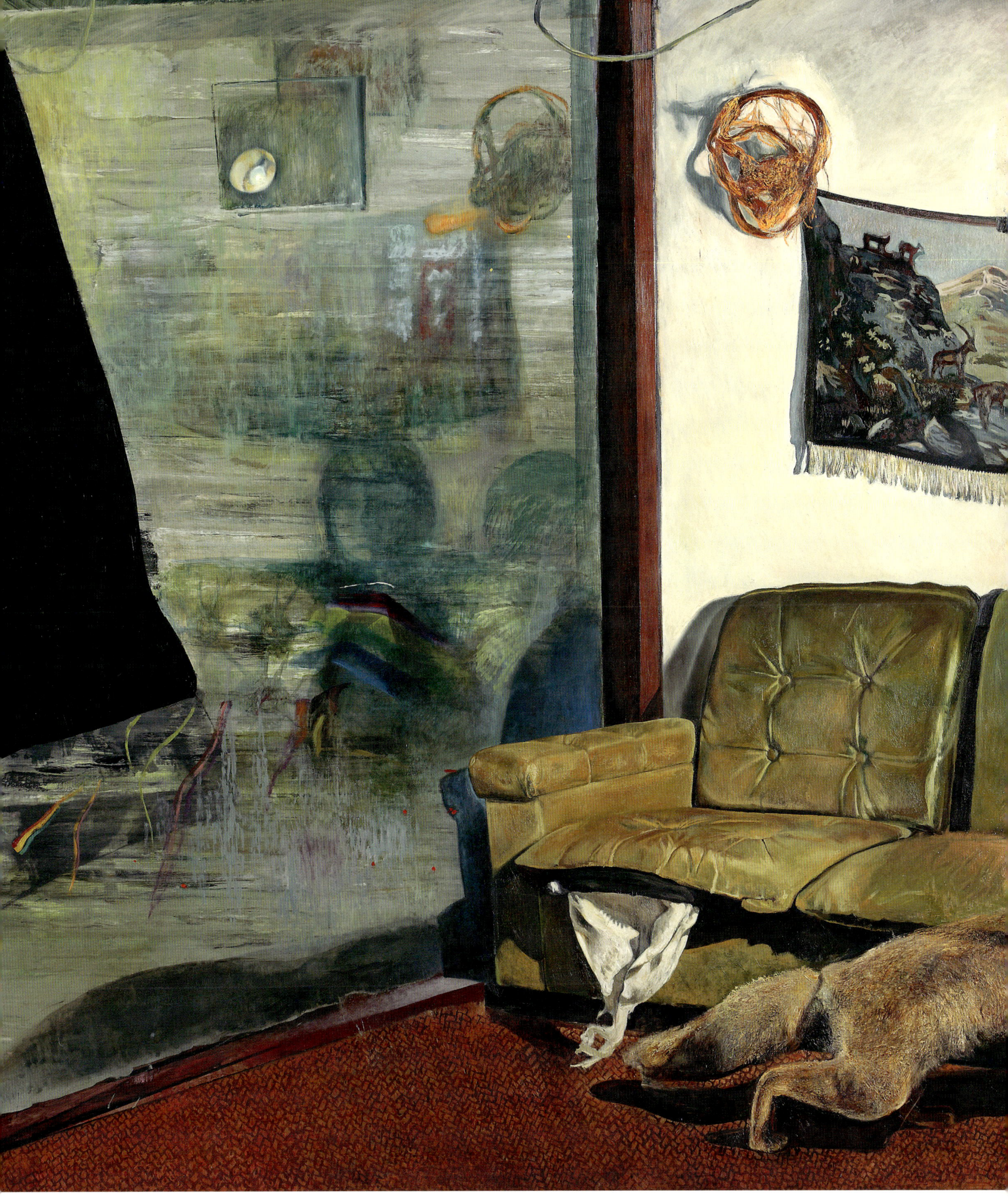

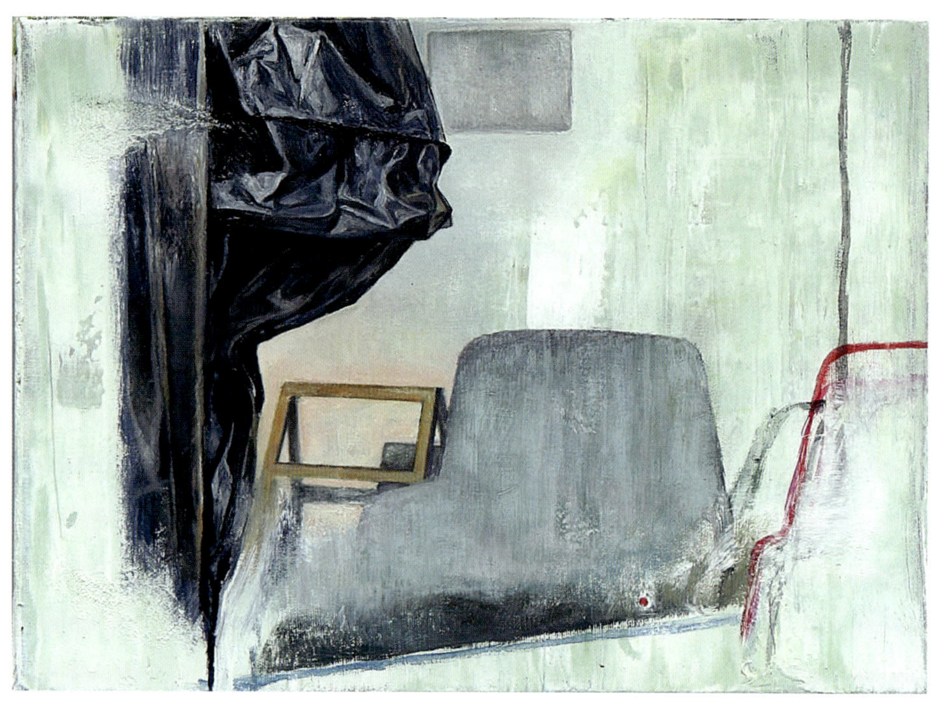

Ohne Titel
2007
30 x 40 cm

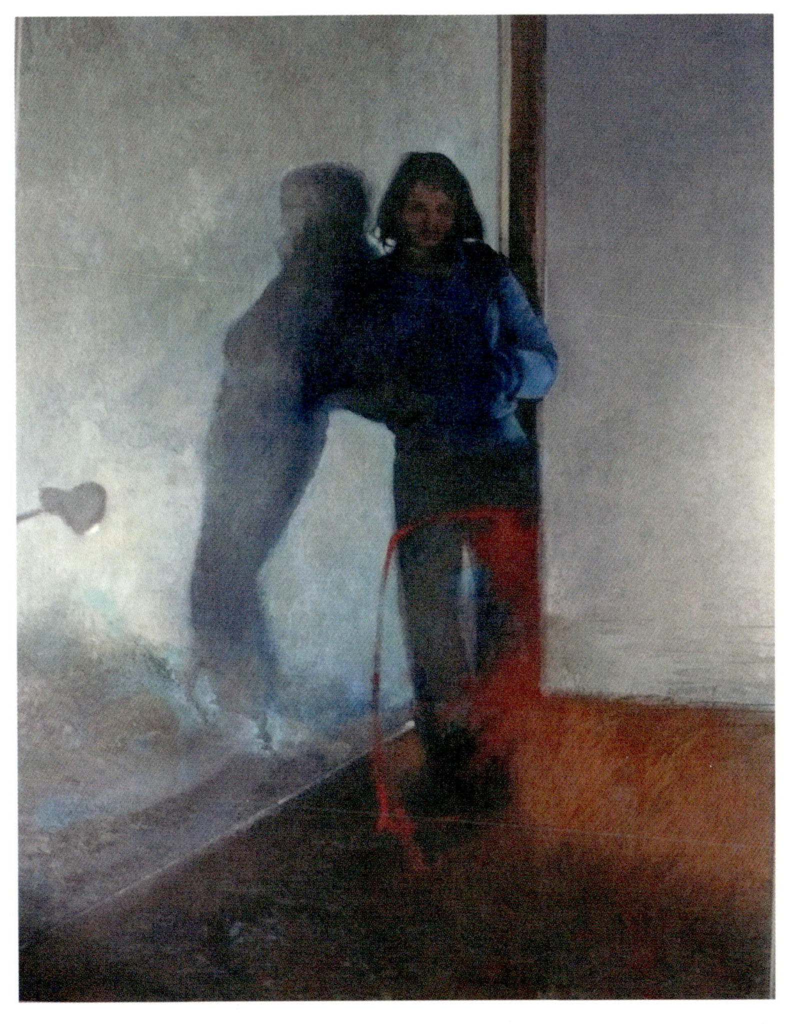

Colour Girl
2007
210 x 160 cm

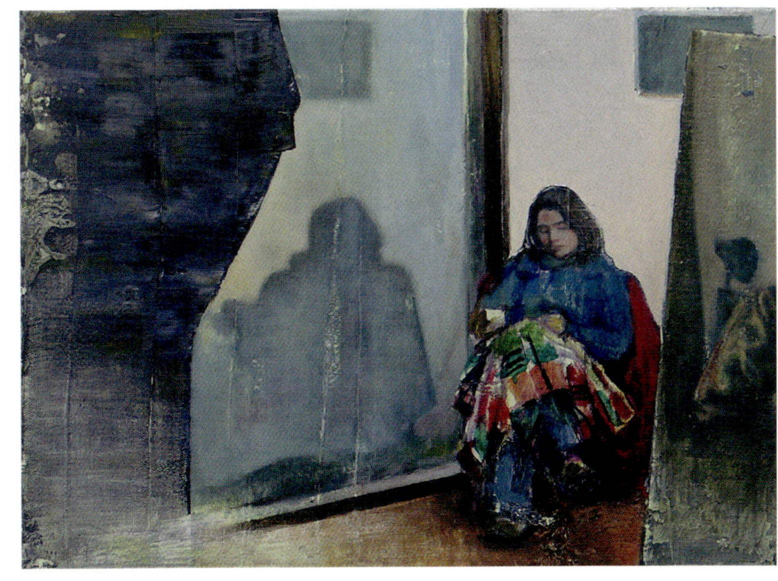

BB
2007
30 x 40 cm

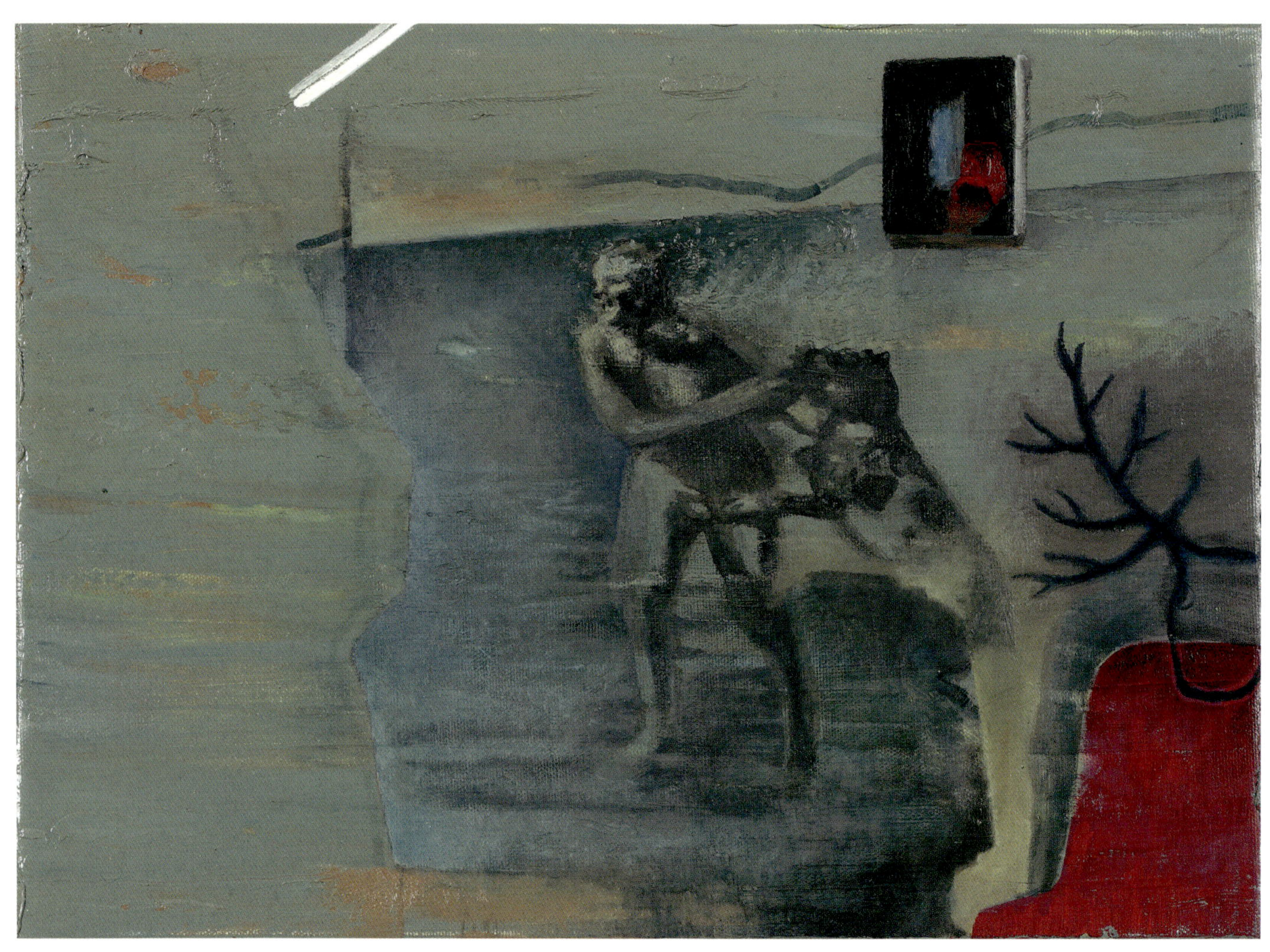

Mary
2007
30 x 40 cm

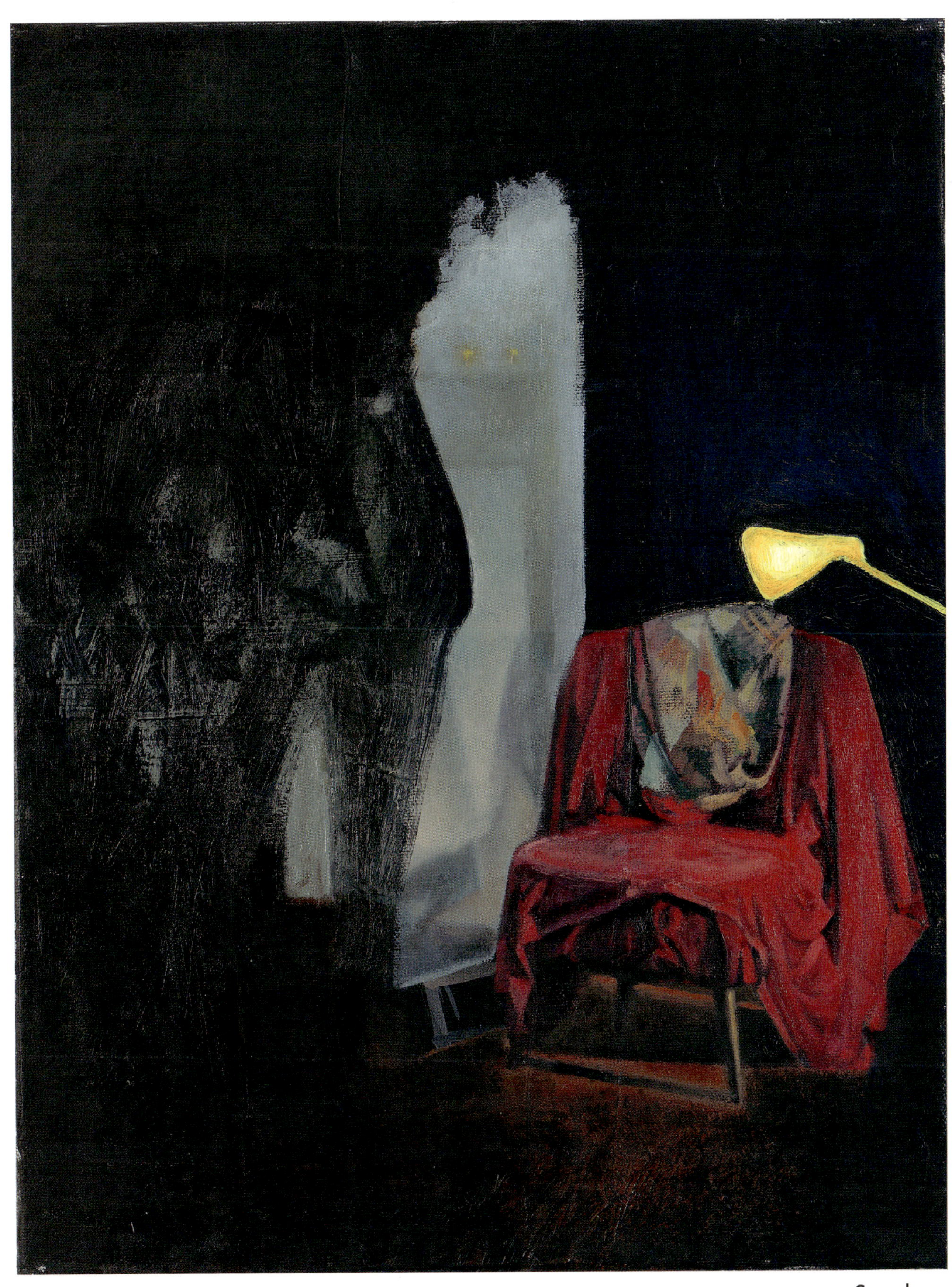

Sessel

2007

40 x 30 cm

Sack
2007
30 x 40 cm

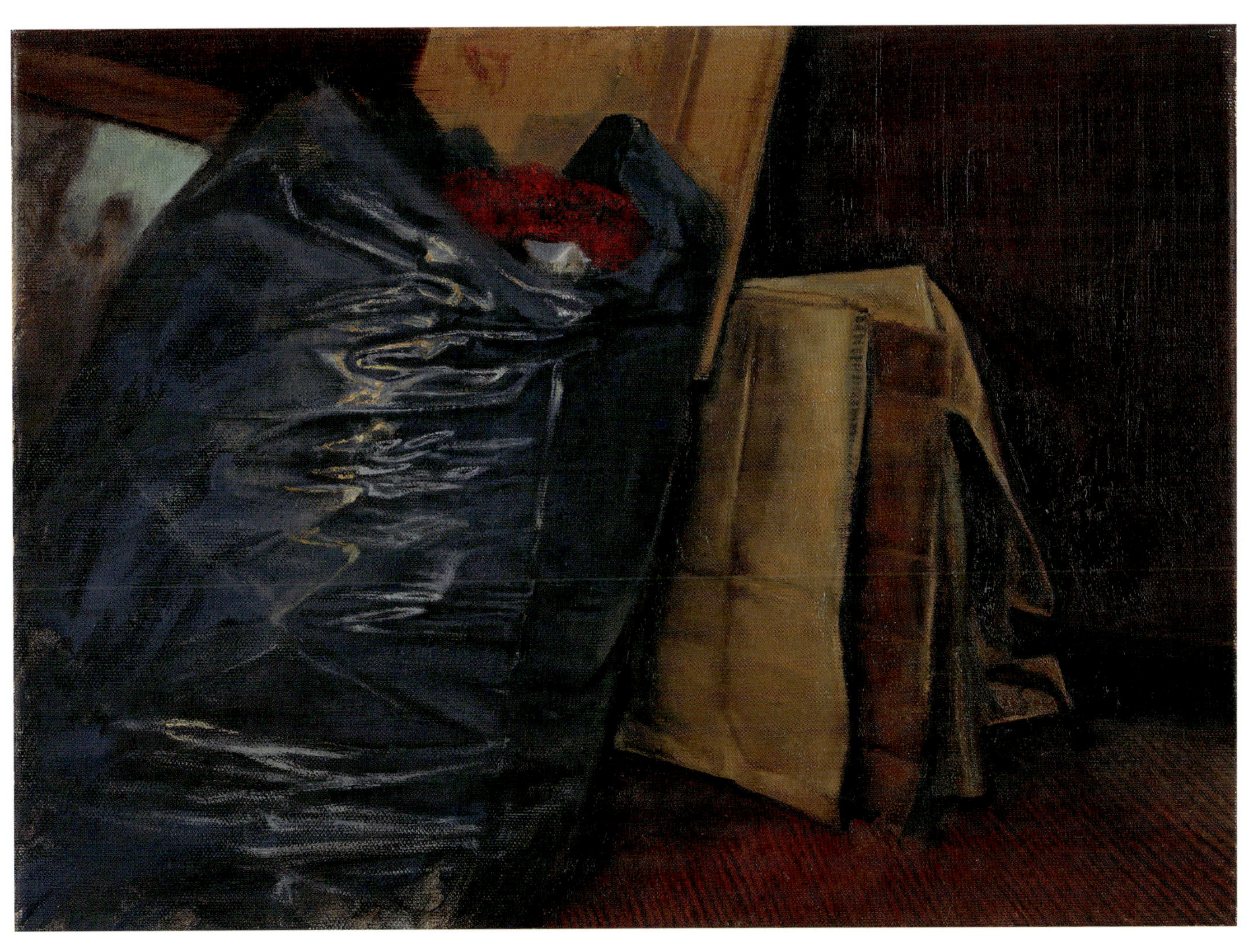

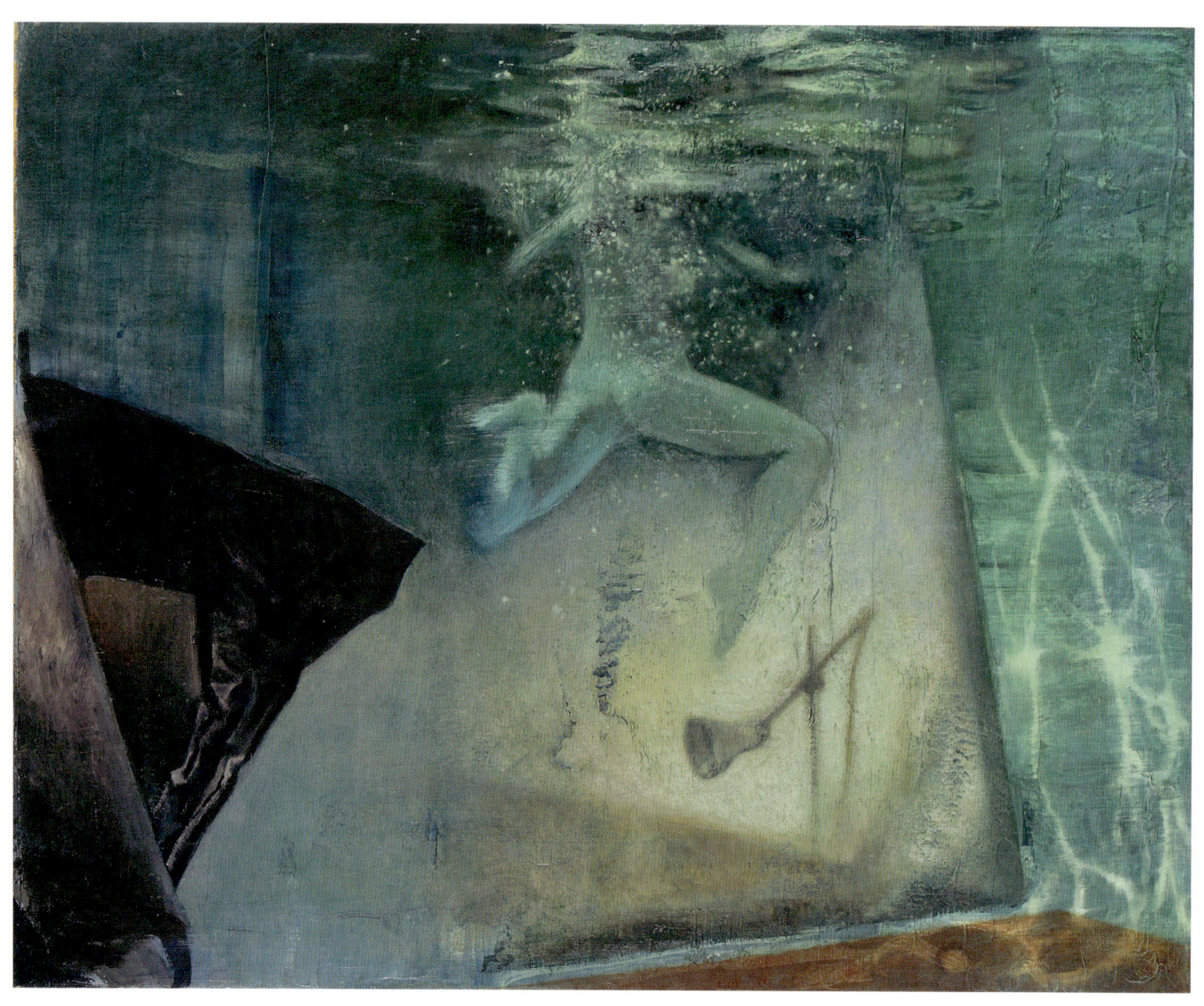

CX
2007
50 x 60 cm

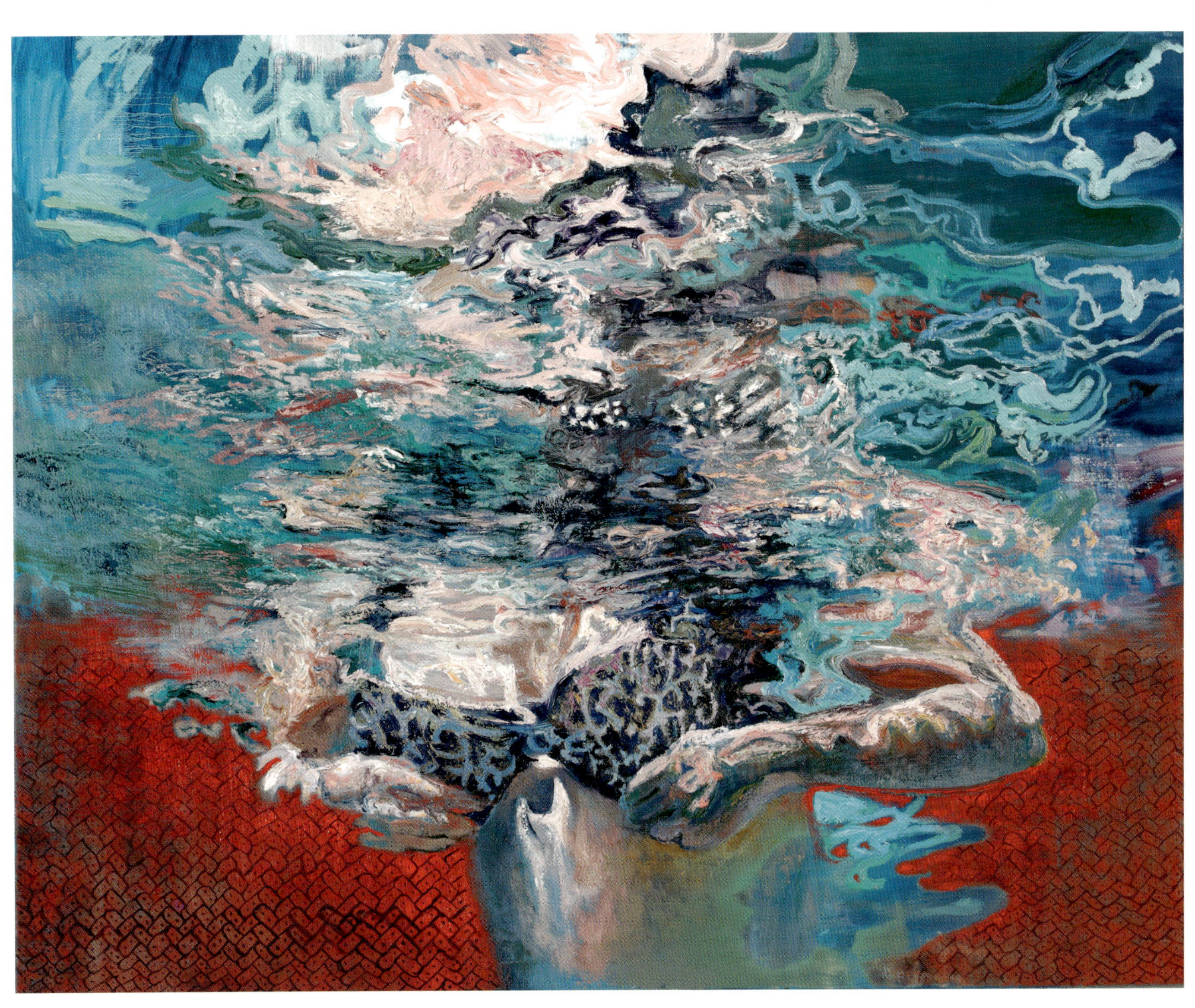

C.
2007
50 x 60 cm

Gordon

2007

90 x 100 cm

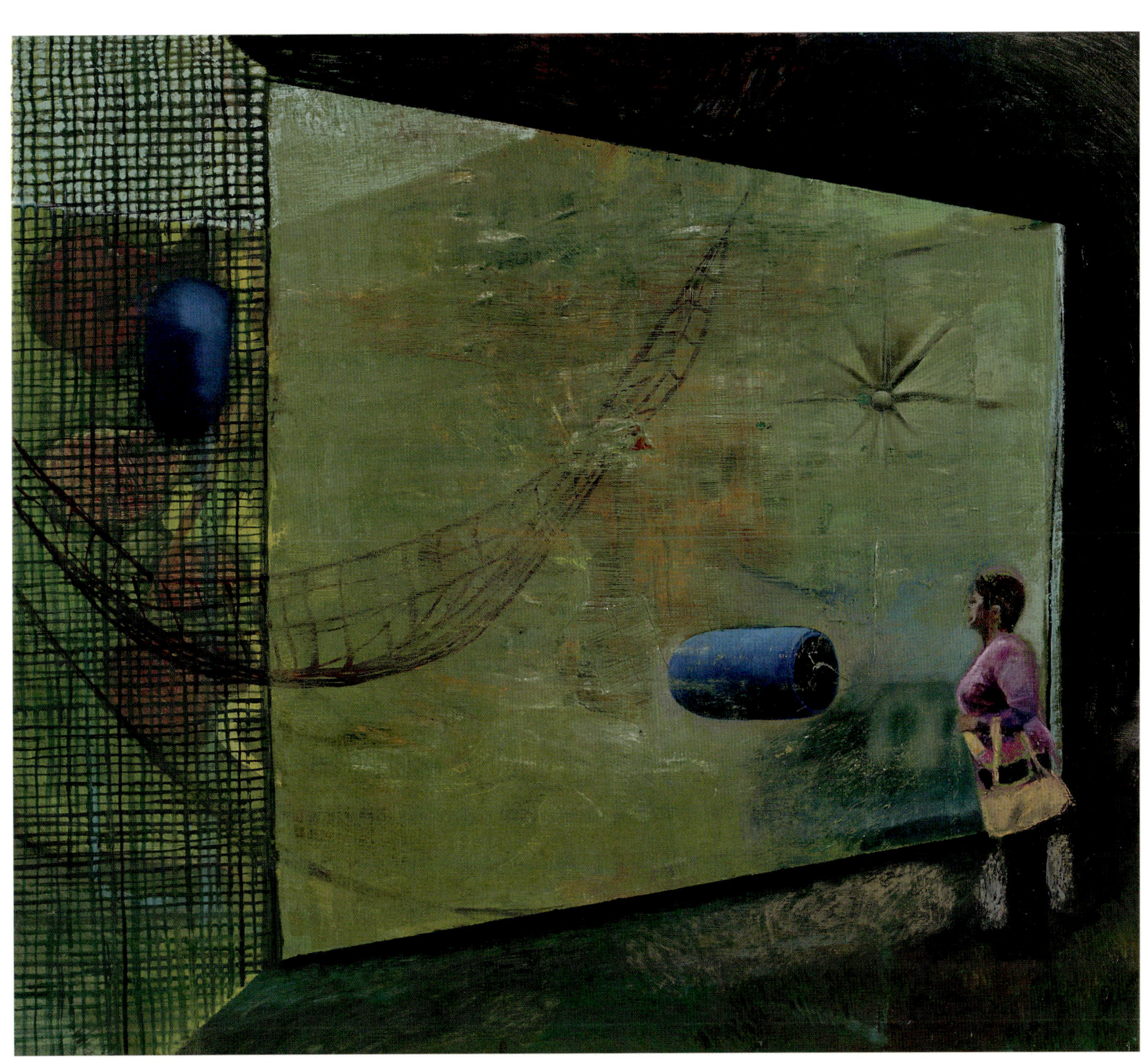

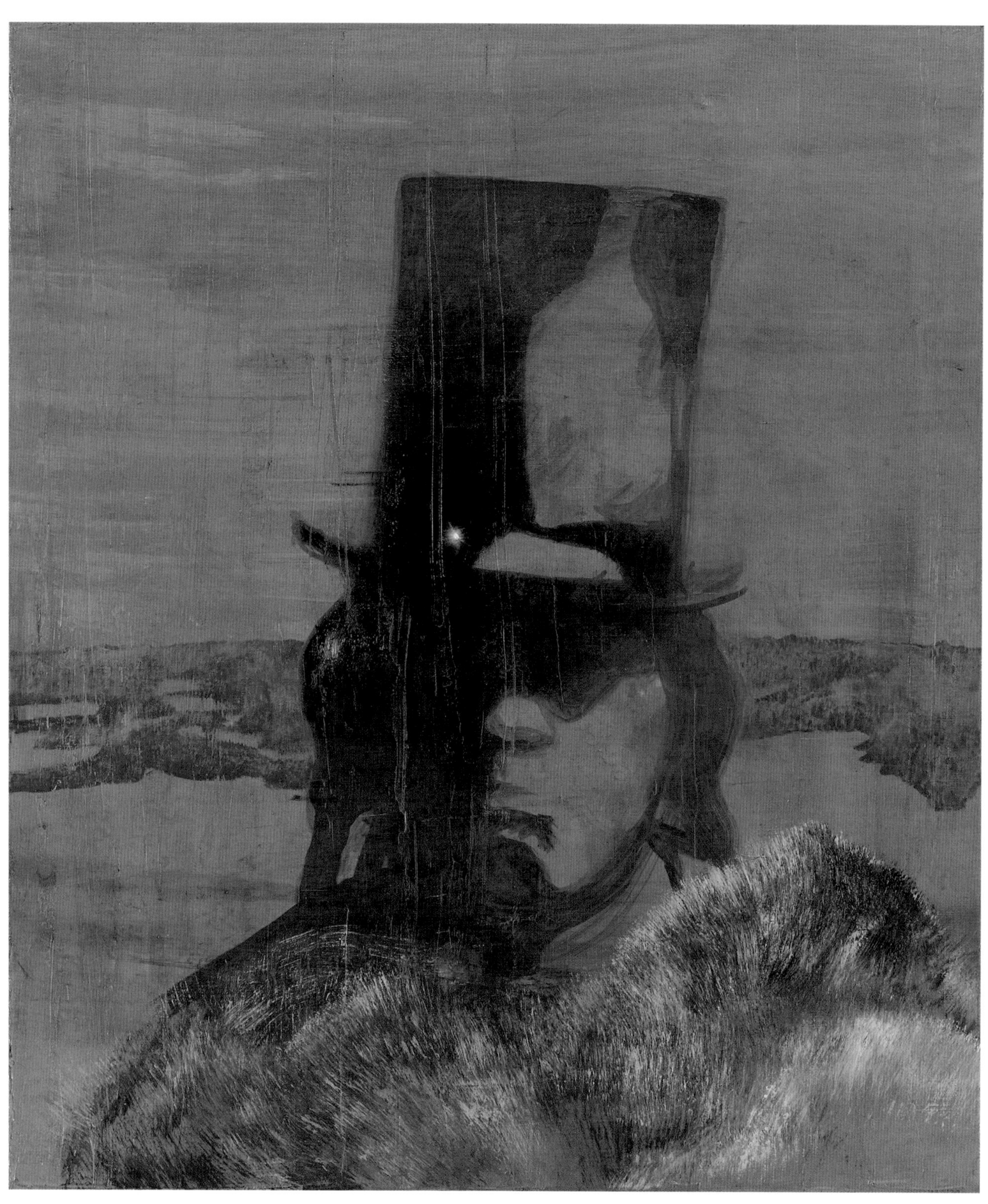

Alexanderschlacht
2008
60 x 50 cm

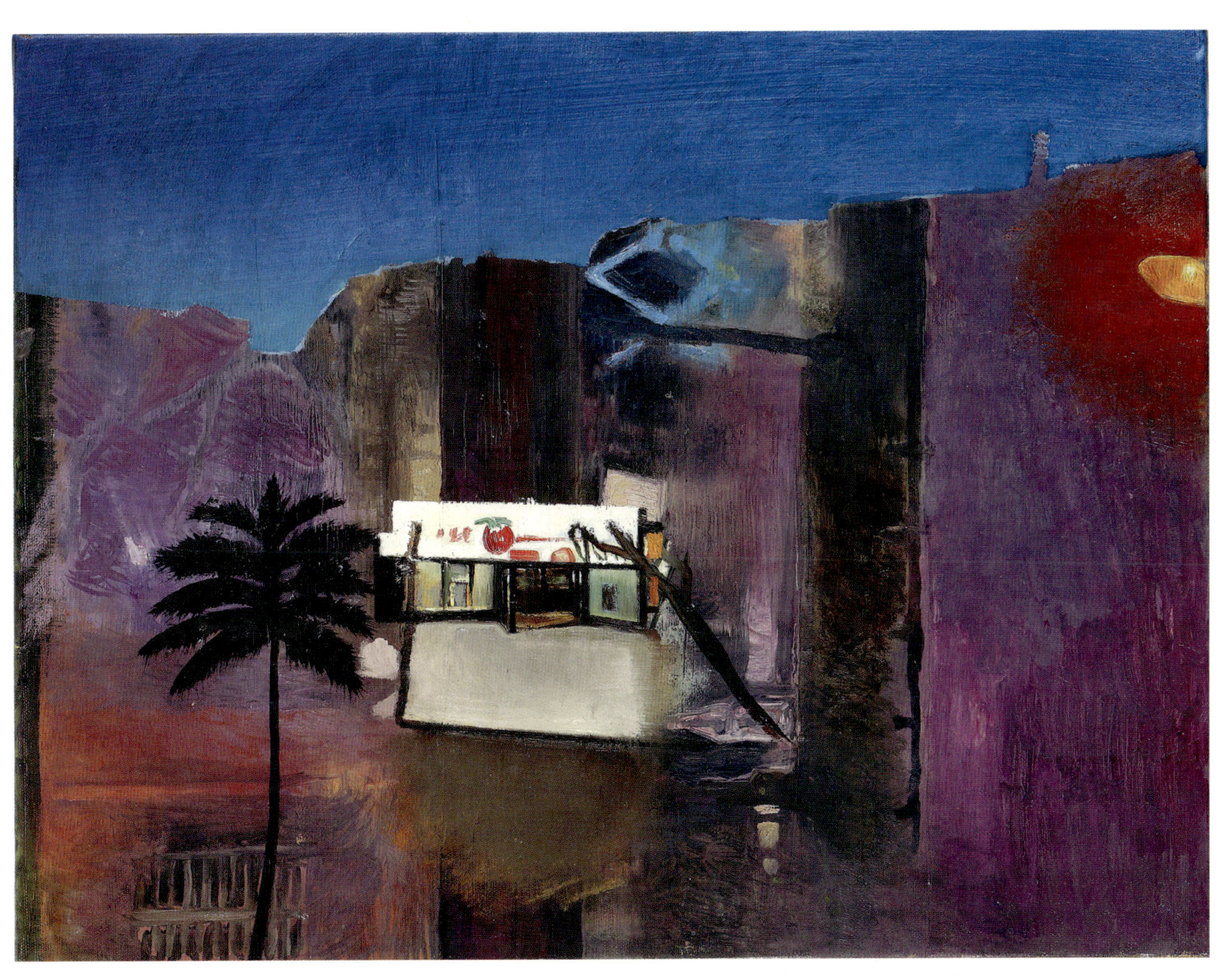

Palm
2007
40 x 50 cm

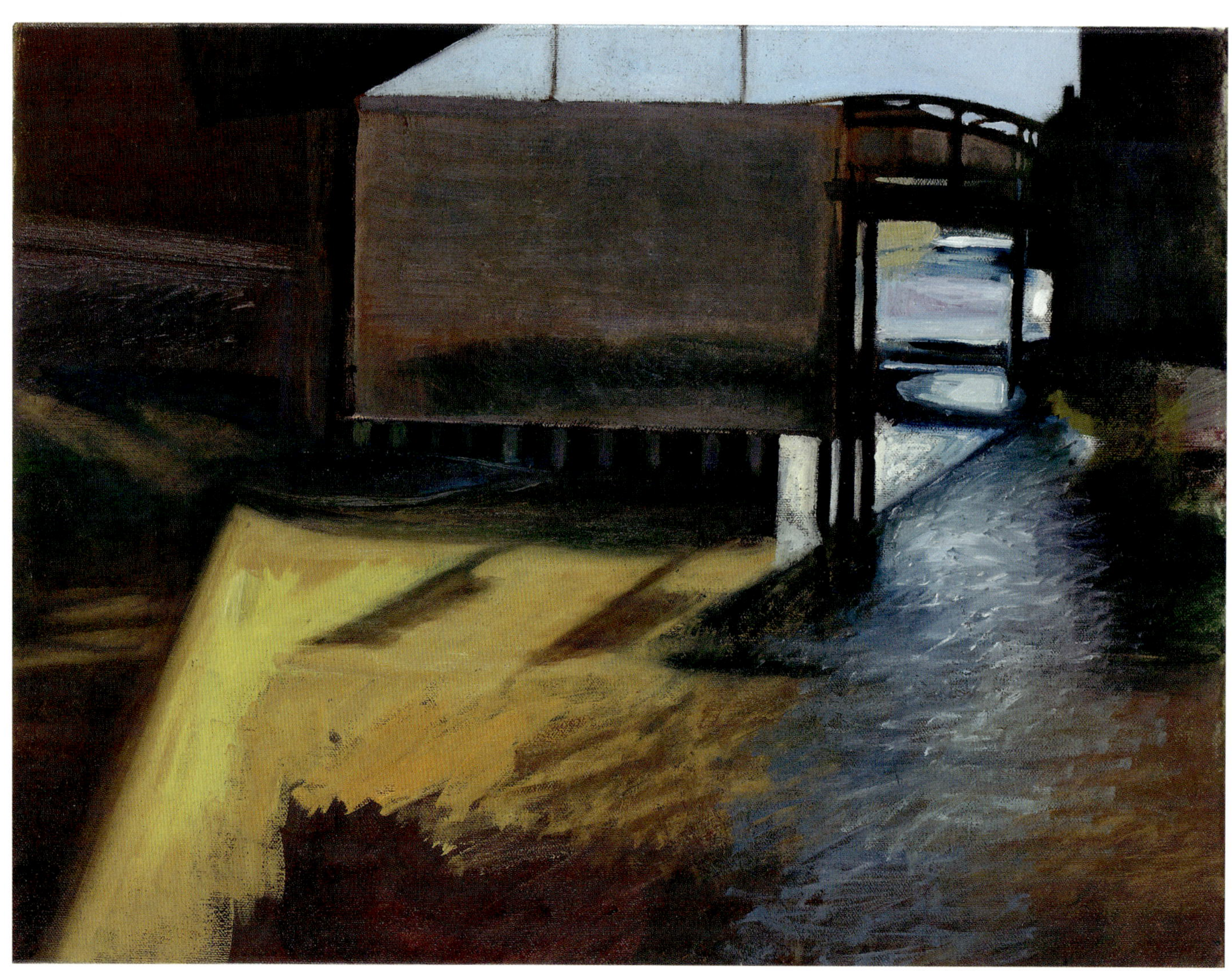

Fahnen
2007
40 x 50 cm

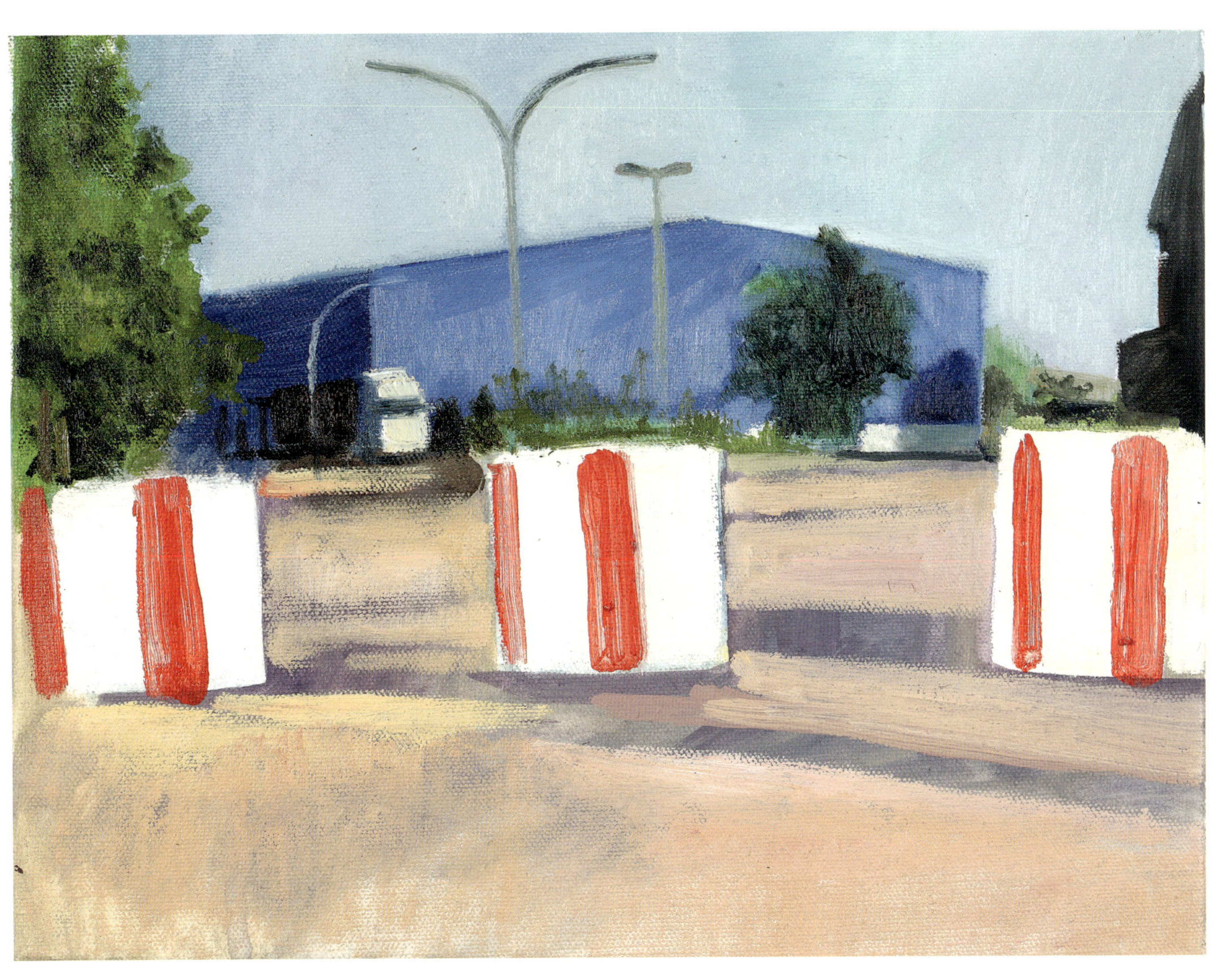

EM
2008
24 x 30 cm

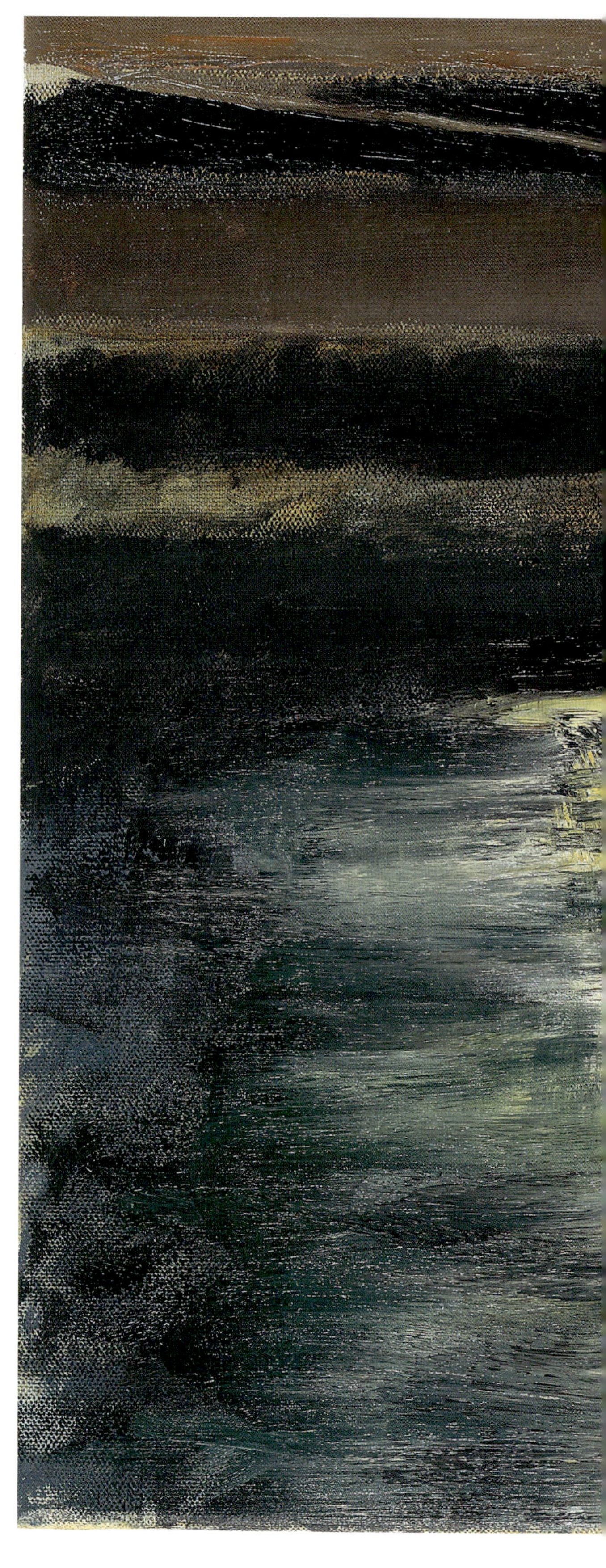

Boot
2007
40 x 50 cm

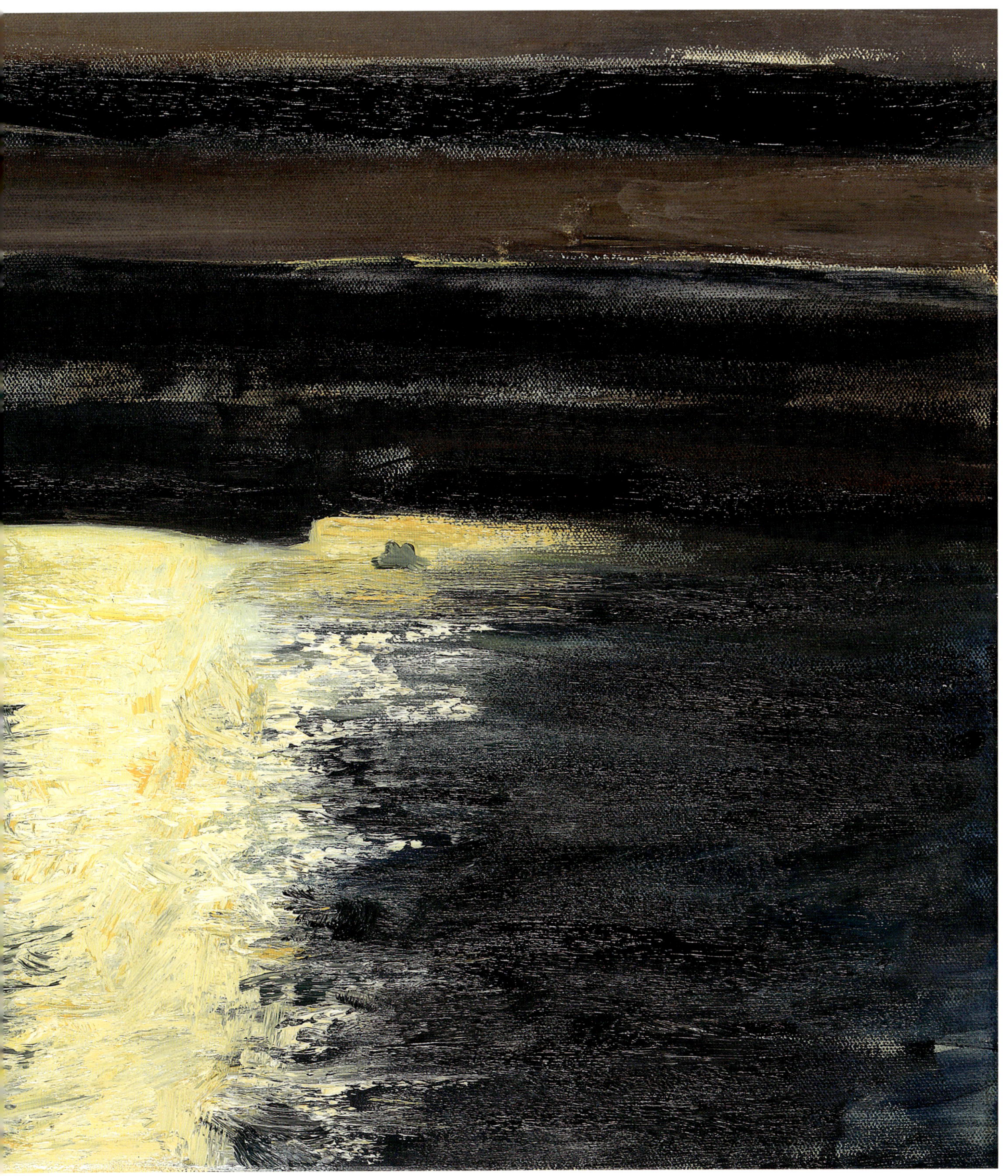

31
Ponton, 2008
Öl auf Leinwand
Oil on canvas
210 x 160 cm

32
Fux, 2008
Öl und Tempera auf Leinwand
Oil and tempera on canvas
70 x 60 cm

33
Reineke, 2008
Öl auf Leinwand
Oil on canvas
60 x 70 cm

34
Pank, 2008
Öl auf Leinwand
Oil on canvas
60 x 50 cm

35
Maske, 2007
Öl und Tempera auf Malpappe
Oil and tempera on paintboard
60 x 50 cm

36/37
Kreis, 2008
Öl auf Leinwand
Oil on canvas
165 x 210 cm

39
Perro, 2008
Öl auf Leinwand
Oil on canvas
90 x 100 cm

41
Ozeanien, 2008
Öl auf Leinwand
Oil on canvas
90 x 100 cm

43
G., 2008
Öl auf Leinwand
Oil on canvas
100 x 90 cm

45
Eco, 2007
Öl und Tempera auf Leinwand
Oil and tempera on canvas
90 x 100 cm

47
Flasche, 2008
Öl auf Leinwand
Oil on canvas
80 x 100 cm

49
Electrick, 2008
Öl auf Leinwand
Oil on canvas
200 x 175 cm

50
Ohne Titel, 2007
Öl und Tempera auf Leinwand
Oil and tempera on canvas
30 x 40 cm
Privatsammlung, Deutschland
Private Collection, Germany

51
Colour Girl, 2007
Öl und Tempera auf Leinwand
Oil and tempera on canvas
210 x 160 cm
Privatsammlung, Deutschland
Private Collection, Germany

51
BB, 2007,
Öl und Tempera auf Leinwand
Oil and tempera on canvas
30 x 40 cm
Privatsammlung, Deutschland
Private Collection, Germany

52
Mary, 2007
Öl und Tempera auf Leinwand
Oil and tempera on canvas
30 x 40 cm

53
Sessel, 2007
Öl und Tempera auf Leinwand
Oil and tempera on canvas
40 x 30 cm

55
Sack, 2007
Öl und Tempera auf Leinwand
Oil and tempera on canvas
30 x 40 cm

56
CX, 2007
Öl und Tempera auf Leinwand
Oil and tempera on canvas
50 x 60 cm

57
C., 2007
Öl und Tempera auf Leinwand
Oil and tempera on canvas
50 x 60 cm

59
Gordon, 2007
Öl auf Leinwand
Oil on canvas
90 x 100 cm

60
Alexanderschlacht, 2008
Öl auf Leinwand
Oil on canvas
60 x 50 cm
Sammlung ASS, Hamburg
ASS Collection, Hamburg

61
Palm, 2007
Öl auf Leinwand
Oil on canvas
40 x 50 cm

62
Fahnen, 2007
Öl und Tempera auf Leinwand
Oil and tempera on canvas
40 x 50 cm

63
EM, 2008
Öl auf Leinwand
Oil on canvas
24 x 30 cm
Privatsammlung, Hamburg
Private Collection, Hamburg

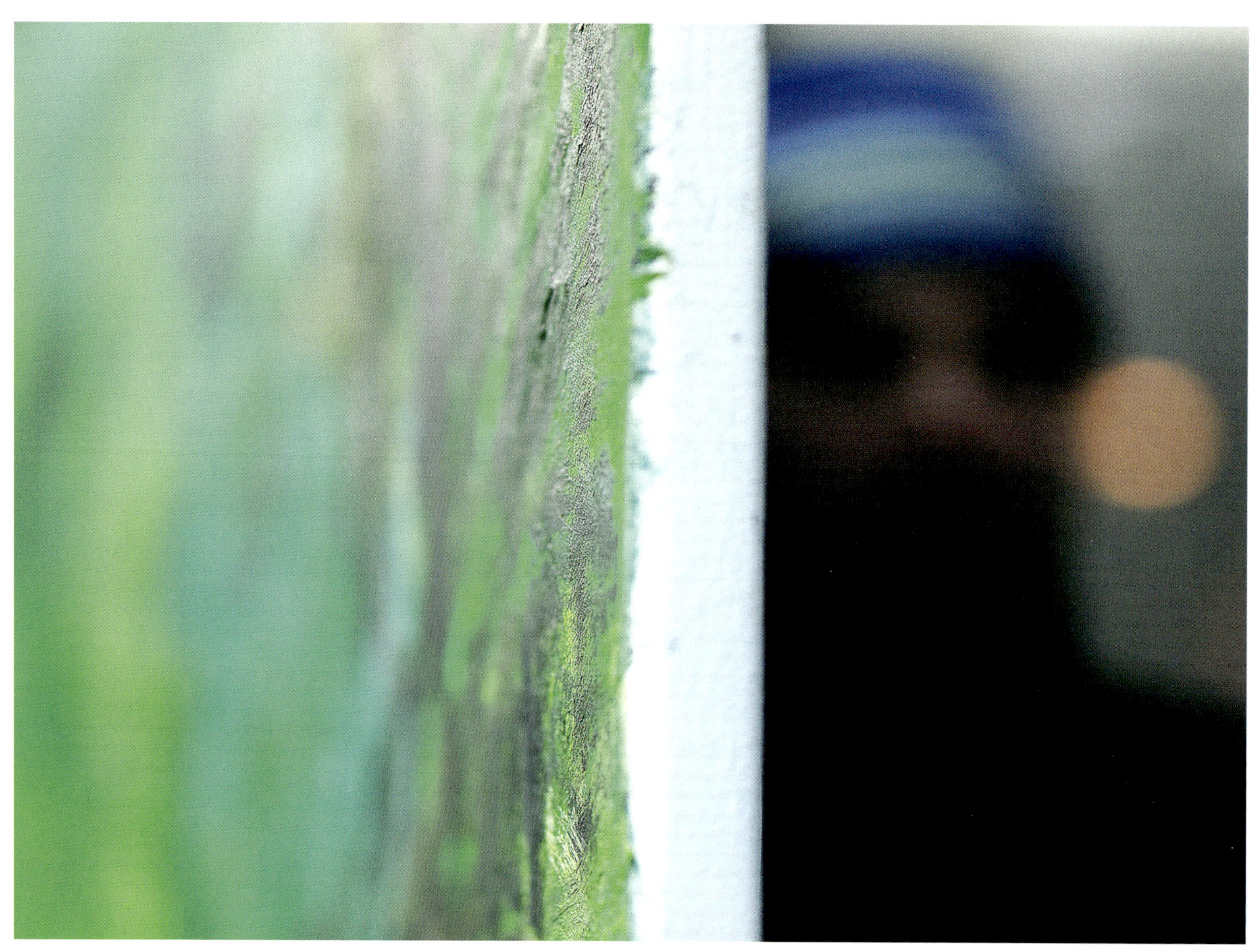

Portrait Alexander Raymond
Photo: Jan Deichner

Alexander Raymond

1970	geboren in Heilbronn

Ausbildung:

1990-92	Universität Heidelberg
1993-94	Kunstschule Rödel, Mannheim
1994-98	Hochschule für Angewandte Wissenschaften (HAW) Hamburg

Ausstellungen:

2008 *ANDERSWO, KONTEMPORÄR*, Hamburg (G)
Sehnsucht Landschaft, Schloß Agathenburg, Agathenburg (G)
ART.FAIR 21 Messe für aktuelle Kunst, Köln, LEVY Galerie Hamburg (G, K)
artparisX, Paris, LEVY Galerie Hamburg (G, K)

2007 ART.FAIR 21 Messe für aktuelle Kunst, Köln, LEVY Galerie Hamburg (G, K)

2006-09 *Marilyn Monroe: Life as a Legend*, Museumswanderausstellung USA & Kanada (G, K)

2006 SKAM im raum 2, Mannheim (G)
Alexander Raymond – Schichten des Wirklichen, Galerie Levy, Hamburg, (E, K)

2004 GalerieXpressns, Hamburg (G)

2003 SKAM, Hamburg (G)

2001 SKAM Finale, Hamburg (G)

1999 Deutsche Bank, Essen (E)
3 CV, Fundbüro Hamburg (G)

1997 *Projektmenge 1*, Kunstverein Eberbach (G)

1994 Galerie Kokotte, Hamburg (E)

E = Einzelausstellung   G = Gruppenausstellung   K = Katalog

1970	born in Heilbronn

Education:

1990–92	Heidelberg University
1993–94	Kunstschule Rödel, Mannheim
1994–98	Hamburg University of Applied Sciences (HAW)

Exhibitions:

2008 *ANDERSWO, KONTEMPORÄR*, Hamburg (G)
Sehnsucht Landschaft, Schloss Agathenburg, Agathenburg (G)
ART.FAIR 21 Messe für aktuelle Kunst, Cologne, LEVY Galerie Hamburg (G, C)
artparisX, Paris, LEVY Galerie Hamburg (G, K)

2007 ART.FAIR 21 Messe für aktuelle Kunst, Cologne, LEVY Galerie Hamburg (G, C)

2006-09 *Marilyn Monroe: Life as a Legend*, museum exhibition touring the USA & Canada (G, C)

2006 SKAM im raum 2, Mannheim (G)
Alexander Raymond – Schichten des Wirklichen, Galerie Levy, Hamburg, (S, C)

2004 GalerieXpressns, Hamburg (G)

2003 SKAM, Hamburg (G)

2001 SKAM Finale, Hamburg (G)

1999 Deutsche Bank, Essen (S)
3 CV, Fundbüro Hamburg (G)

1997 *Projektmenge 1*, Kunstverein Eberbach (G)

1994 Galerie Kokotte, Hamburg (S)

S = Solo exhibition   G = Group exhibition   C = Catalog

Impressum | Colophon

Diese Publikation erscheint anlässlich der Ausstellungen:
This publication was produced to accompany the exhibition:

Alexander Raymond – ABNOE
13. 1. – 19. 2. 2009
LEVY Galerie, Hamburg

5. 2009
Westwendischer Kunstverein e.V.
Zehntspeicher, 29471 Gartow/Quarnstedt

Herausgeber / Produced by:
LEVY Galerie Hamburg
Osterfeldstrasse 6
D-22529 Hamburg
T.: +49 40 45 91 88
F.: +49 40 44 72 25
info@galerie-levy.de
www.galerie-levy.de

Texte / Essays:
Jens Asthoff, Hamburg
Nora Sdun, Hamburg

Redaktion / Editing:
Alexander Sairally, Hamburg

Übersetzung / Translations:
Sean Gallagher, Nanaimo, BC
Gillian Morris, Berlin

Photonachweis / Photo credits:
Dirk Masbaum, Hamburg
Jan Deichner, Freiburg (Portrait)

Grafische Gestaltung / Graphic design:
Alexander Raymond, Klaus-Peter Plehn, Alexander Sairally

Die Deutsche Nationalbibliothek verzeichnet diese Publikation
in der Deutschen Nationalbibliografie; detaillierte biblio-
grafische Daten sind im Internet über http://dnb.ddb.de
abrufbar. / The Deutsche Nationalbibliothek holds a record of
this publication in the Deutsche Nationalbibliografie; detailed
bibliographical data can be found under: http://dnb.ddb.de.

Gesamtherstellung und Vertrieb /
Published and distributed by:
Kerber Verlag, Bielefeld
Windelsbleicher Str. 166–170
33659 Bielefeld
Germany
Tel. +49 (0) 5 21/9 50 08-10
Fax +49 (0) 5 21/9 50 08-88
E-Mail: info@kerberverlag.com
www.kerberverlag.com

Kerber, US Distribution
D.A.P., Distributed Art Publishers Inc.
155 Sixth Avenue 2nd Floor
New York, N. Y. 10013
Tel. +1 212 6 27-19 99
Fax +1 212 6 27-94 84

© 2009 Kerber Verlag Bielefeld, Alexander Raymond,
Jens Asthoff, Nora Sdun, Dirk Masbaum, LEVY Galerie

ISBN 978-3-86678-249-5

Printed in Germany